# *Eight Years in the Amazon Headwaters*

## *My Life in Three Peruvian Tribes*

*by*

## Lila Wistrand Robinson

authorHOUSE™

*1663 LIBERTY DRIVE, SUITE 200*
*BLOOMINGTON, INDIANA 47403*
*(800) 839-8640*
*WWW.AUTHORHOUSE.COM*

© 2005 Lila Wistrand Robinson. All Rights Reserved.

*No part of this book may be reproduced, stored in a retrieval system, or transmitted by any means without the written permission of the author.*

*First published by AuthorHouse 05/19/05*

ISBN: 1-4208-3493-2 (sc)

*Library of Congress Control Number: 2005901653*

*Printed in the United States of America*
*Bloomington, Indiana*

*This book is printed on acid-free paper.*

# CONTENTS

ACKNOWLEDGMENTS ................................................................ vii

**PART I: BACKGROUND AND PREPARATIONS** ................1
CHAPTER 1: PREPARING TO LEAVE.............................2
CHAPTER 2: OFF TO PERU ..............................................7

**PART II: SHAPRA-CANDOSHI TRIBE** ................................13
CHAPTER 3: FIRST SHAPRA TRIBAL EXPERIENCE ............15
CHAPTER 4: FOOD AND COOKING IN THE SHAPRA TRIBE ......................................................................22
CHAPTER 5: CONTINUING LIFE IN THE SHAPRA TRIBE ...24
CHAPTER 6: SECOND TRIP TO THE SHAPRA TRIBE .........31
CHAPTER 7: THE ANACONDA ATTACK ..............................36
CHAPTER 8: LIFE AFTER THE ANACONDA ATTACK .........42

**PART III: THE AGUARUNA TRIBE** ......................................45
CHAPTER 9: FIRST TRIP TO THE AGUARUNA TRIBE .........47
CHAPTER 10: SECOND TRIP TO THE AGUARUNA TRIBE .66
CHAPTER 11: THE TRIP DOWNRIVER ON A RAFT .............69
CHAPTER 12: BACK TO NAZARET .......................................76
CHAPTER 13: THIRD TRIP TO THE AGUARUNA TRIBE ......90
CHAPTER 14: DEATH, FEAR, AND EPIDEMIC ....................97

**PART IV: CASHIBO-CACATAIBO** .....................................109
CHAPTER 15: ASSIGNED TO THE CASHIBO-CACATAIBO TRIBE ............................................................................112
CHAPTER 16: OUR FIRST TRIP TO THE TRIBE ................117
CHAPTER 17: UPRIVER ON THE AGUAYTIA .....................126
CHAPTER 18: TRIP TO THE SAN ALEJANDRO RIVER ......133
CHAPTER 19: SECOND TRIP TO THE AGUAYTIA RIVER..137
CHAPTER 20: THE YEAR 1960 ............................................158
CHAPTER 21: FURLOUGH ...................................................165
CHAPTER 22: BEGINNING MY SECOND TERM .................167
CHAPTER 23: WORKING WITH PEOPLE FROM ANOTHER MISSION .......................................................................170

CHAPTER 24: TRIP TO SUNGARO ..........................................173
CHAPTER 25: WITH A NURSE AS TEMPORARY
PARTNER..................................................................................177
CHAPTER 26: REVISING THE CASHIBO GOSPEL OF
MARK ......................................................................................178

**PART V: UPDATES ON THE THREE TRIBES ....................181**
CHAPTER 27: UPDATE ON THE CANDOSHI.....................182
CHAPTER 28: UPDATE ON THE AGUARUNA.....................192
CHAPTER 29: UPDATE ON THE CACATAIBO WORK........200
EPILOGUE................................................................................205
BIBLIOGRAPHY......................................................................209

# *ACKNOWLEDGMENTS*

This book has been written with the help of various workers in all three tribes. Basic to the first two tribes, Shapra-Candoshi and Aguaruna, were the diaries I kept, written in short, cryptic sentences which needed filling out from memory of the events. Loretta Doris Anderson (Lorrie) gave suggestions for the section on the Shapra area of the Candoshi. She also provided added information for Chapter 7, The Anaconda Attack, with more details than I knew since it was her experience. John and Sheila Tuggy made available letters and information for the Candoshi Update section.

For the Aguaruna tribe, Dr. Mildred Larson's book *Treasures in Clay Pots* was a helpful source of information about her Aguaruna New Testament translation. Dennis Olson provided information and pictures for the Aguaruna Update. All other pictures were taken by me. Jeanne Grover's unpublished paper "Land Development Among the Aguarunas" was also referenced.

James and Gloria Gray Wroughton provided statistics on the life of Dr. Olive Shell in the Cashibo-Cacataibo Update. Irma Schaal Sawdon graciously provided her letters to her parents giving information about the two years we worked together in that tribe.

Thanks go to my sister Barbara Wistrand Whitman for editing the complete manuscript and making many improvements. Many thanks go to Dan Smith for help in computerizing this book.

# PART I: BACKGROUND AND PREPARATIONS

# CHAPTER 1: PREPARING TO LEAVE

New Year's day of 1956 started at five o'clock in the morning when I dressed, gathered my luggage, and hurried to the Houston airport where thirty friends and relatives were waiting. I was given a beautiful orchid for this special goodbye. Two teen-agers, Sue Bell and Cora Lynn Pollock, were dressed up in clownish outfits to lighten our spirits and had collected money for me to spend on the way to my destination. I boarded the airplane which would take me to Miami and on to Peru, South America, where I would be assigned to a tribe of Native Americans in the broad rain forest. It was a pivotal day in my life, a day etched in my memory.

What had brought me to this point of wanting to live in a foreign country with primitive, indigenous people? Why was I willing to learn the ways of those people about whom I knew nothing? How did I arrive at this willingness to leave my comfortable homeland?

My brother Kent was taking Spanish courses at the University of Houston while I studied Spanish in high school for two years. Together, we listened to Spanish language radio programs in Houston. We immensely enjoyed learning the language; seeing how words and phrases changed and, yet, were the same in different languages. Combining this with hearing missionary speakers at church telling about their experiences in Latin America, we both felt called to missions in Latin America. At Camp Peniel campfire services, we both threw small cuttings of tree branches into the campfire symbolizing our willingness to let our lives burn brightly in service for God. After high school, my brother Kent went to Dallas Bible Institute (DBI) where he heard speakers from Wycliffe Bible Translators (WBT) tell of translating the New Testament into languages of tribal peoples in Latin America. After finishing high school, I also went to DBI. After his graduation, Kent was drafted into the army and went to fight in the Korean conflict. I graduated from DBI in 1953 and went to the Summer Institute of Linguistics (SIL) at the University of Oklahoma in 1954. SIL teaches university courses in linguistics and anthropology as well as publishes technical articles in the fields of linguistics and anthropology. The courses were difficult, but I had a knack for learning languages and enjoyed the studies. At SIL I practiced by learning Kiowa, a Native American language of Oklahoma, and working with Kiowa consultants who patiently taught me their language. During that summer of study, I prayed about joining SIL and its sister institution WBT. I went through the process of application and was accepted to work in Peru. In 1958, Kent also went to SIL in Oklahoma and joined SIL/WBT to work in Mexico. I was excited with anticipation of working with SIL International (SIL), the organization responsible for fieldwork, and WBT, the organization with the vision of seeing lives changed through Bible translation.

After my acceptance into these institutions, I began to gather equipment for "boot camp", which we also called "jungle camp." The people at my home church had enthusiastically worked to help me obtain equipment such as a duffel bag, a machete, sneakers, a mosquito net, an air mattress, and a sleeping bag. I would be using my compiled equipment for at least five years or more. After all my needs were gathered and packed, I left Houston on January 1, 1955. My former SIL roommate, Jean Shand, and I met in San Antonio and traveled into Mexico. We rode the train to Mexico City, then took a bus to the city of Tuxtla in the southern state of Chiapas. The bus ride was sporadic, since the engine of the bus needed fixing at various times along the way. In Oaxaca City, the driver drove around the city seeking scarce gasoline so we could continue on our way. We arrived in Tuxtla, disheveled, hungry, and exhausted, nine hours late. The pilot of the Missionary Aviation Fellowship (MAF) met us at the belated bus. He and his wife let us stay at their home to catch up on our sleep. The next day he flew us out to boot camp in a small, single-engine plane. The flight was spectacular over steep, forest-covered mountains. Finally, we arrived at a small settlement of grass-thatched huts, some for us campers, but also an administration building, dining room, kitchen, and classrooms. Jean and I were assigned to one of the huts where we unpacked our sleeping gear and mosquito net. There was an earthen floor into which the pole legs of our primitive beds had been driven.

We had classes in how to do medical work in tropical areas, including giving injections. To learn to give injections we first practiced on thin-skinned oranges. After doing that several times, we practiced on our classmates. We were taught to always pull back the plunger of the syringe to be sure the needle was not in a vein or artery. Those were the days when syringes were washed in detergent and water, then boiled to sterilize them for re-use. Later in my tribal experiences in Peru, I used this knowledge in giving many injections, mainly in the buttocks, to old and young alike.

We also studied how to understand the working of engines since each World War II radio we used would be powered by a Briggs and Stratton engine. We were taught how to handle a canoe, whether poling or steering. One camper was steering a canoe through some small rapids, but lost control and went toward the bank where low-hanging trees swept him off the back. He was bobbing in the river, but found his way to shore while his partner gained control of the runaway canoe. We built up our strength by hiking first just short distances, then finally a fifty-mile round trip to see the Lacandon, a Maya tribe. They were a small group of people who lived on food harvested from their gardens. Men and women wore loose, dress-like robes. Setting on a shelf were god-pots, small pottery bowls that they worshipped.

I learned to swim using the sidestroke. The final test in swimming was to swim across the Jataté River to a sand beach. I started out fine, but when I came to the main strong current it started carrying me downriver around a curve. The swim teacher, who was waiting on the sand beach, dived in to pull me onto the shore safely. I had made it three-fourths of the way across by myself. None of us were used to so much intensive out-door exercise, and our appetites ballooned. I gained ten pounds while in boot camp.

The base camp was built in a clearing in the midst of a tropical forest area. After our training at the base camp, we were taken to small clearings in the forest where two by two we were to build a thatched hut and the furniture in it. Pat Baptista was my *"champa mate"*, as the huts were called. We had the help of a couple of native men who thatched the roof on a log frame they made. We then set about making furniture such as our two beds, a table, and a stove, out of cane poles, vine, and local materials. The beds were not difficult to put together with materials the men cut to size, but the mud stove

*Background and Preparations*

was a real challenge. With cane pole framing, we formed the front of the stove wider than the back, applying thick mud which hardened nicely when the fire was built. The top of the stove was made from a flattened metal cracker can, and a couple of food tins on top of one another served as a smokestack at the back of the stove. After the rudimentary furniture was built, we had only a small amount of basic food items rationed to us so we would learn to live on local food as much as possible. Later, in our tribal assignments we would only be able to take a small amount of canned food, flour, sugar, and salt with us. Partner Pat Baptista was later assigned to a tribe in Bolivia. Boot camp was invaluable training that I would draw upon often during my years in the rain forest of Peru.

After boot camp I went to the Oaxaca Chontal tribe of Mexico, accompanied by Jeanne Miller of Pennsylvania. We were flown to the city of Salina Cruz where we spent the night with a missionary family. Since we were near the Pacific Ocean, we could hear the strong waves crashing on the shore. The next afternoon we left Salina Cruz, flying about two hours north along the Pacific coast. Below us we saw salt being harvested from the pools of ocean water. We landed near the ocean, unloaded our duffel bags, and began the hour's walking trip to the village where linguist Viola Waterhouse and SIL friend Myra Johnson would be our hostesses. We walked over a hill accompanied by Oaxaca Chontal women dressed in *huipil* blouses with long skirts, and carrying water pots on their heads. A *huipil* blouse is made of cotton cloth with colorful, red and yellow heavy sewing machine stitching in front and back making it very durable. An ox-drawn cart carried our luggage. At the top of the hill we could see the distant village stretched out in the valley before us. As the sun dipped below the horizon and as darkness enveloped us, we neared the town where we could see kerosene lights and candles twinkling in the doorways and windows. This would be home to us for two months as we experienced what it would be like to live in a minority culture of Mexico where the Oaxaca Chontal language was spoken. We wore the native blouses, long skirts and sandals to fit into the local culture.

We four single women (Viola, Myra, Jeanne, and I) were staying in a two-room apartment, consisting of kitchen and bedroom. Viola,

*Eight Years in the Amazon Headwaters*

called "Vi", slept in a hammock in the kitchen, and the three of us slept on three single cots in the combination bedroom and living room. During our stay we witnessed a wedding and funeral in the Chontal culture. In the wedding everyone dressed in their very best native clothing and had a fiesta with everyone partying. The funeral service was in the cathedral, followed by a parade to the cemetery headed by a small band playing funeral songs. The two months with the Chontal passed by quickly, and soon it was time to return to the United States for our second summer of SIL linguistics, anthropology, and translation classes at the University of Oklahoma. There I was good friends with Pat Baptista, Ruth Wallen, my future partner and SIL roommate Irma Schaal, and Jeanne Miller. After SIL training was completed, I bought equipment and packed it into fifty-gallon barrels to send to Peru, my assigned country, by boat.

# *CHAPTER 2: OFF TO PERU*

After leaving Houston, I arrived in Miami and was met by friends I had known in Dallas. After an enjoyable afternoon and evening of revisiting old times over a mouth-watering dinner, I crawled into bed for a short night of sleep. After only three hours of sleep, I met six other departing SIL/WBT friends at the Miami airport. Leaving our beloved country at four o'clock in the morning, we conversed a while on the plane about our future adventures before crossing that gulf between two such different cultures. Sleep was the best bridge between the two, and we slept until seven o'clock. We made a brief stop at Tegucigalpa, Honduras, flying on to Managua, Nicaragua, to arrive at 9:30 in the morning. After a half-hour rest, we boarded the plane again, flying to Guayaquil, Ecuador, in five hours. On our last leg of the journey, we flew five more hours to arrive in Lima, the capital of Peru. The whole trip took eighteen hours in a two-engine propeller airplane. Several SIL members met us at the airport and presented flowers to us. Lima was called "the city of parks and flowers". We went quickly through customs, then on to the SIL/WBT Group House, where we were welcomed by the manager, Mrs. Cudney, and ate some delicious Peruvian ice cream. We were assigned rooms and fell into bed, exhausted.

Among the SIL members arriving in Peru with me was Irma Schaal from Iowa, who was to be my partner to work in whatever tribe to which we would be assigned. On January third after breakfast, our group went downtown to fill out papers at the U.S. Embassy. In the afternoon we took a long tour of Lima, at that time having only about a million population. We toured the President's palace, the University of San Marcos, and the central Cathedral where we saw a casket alleged to contain the body of Francisco Pizarro, conqueror of Peru. In later years, however, the casket was removed since the body was most likely not Pizarro's. We toured various, well-known parks and finally upper class San Isidro and other suburbs. Later, a group of us went to the catacombs below a cathedral in downtown Lima. It was late in the afternoon, and we were experiencing the sorrow of the inquisition as we viewed the bones of evangelical Christians who had been killed for their beliefs. Their bones were in deep, wide pits on either side of us as we walked on a narrow pathway flanked by the six-foot drop down to the bones. After spending at least an hour down there musing about the death of the believers, we were shocked when the lights went off. We were afraid to move, for we would tumble down to the bones. We called out loudly for a few minutes, then breathed a sigh of relief when the lights came back on. We hurried back to the entrance and departed just as the catacombs were being locked for the day.

A few days after our arrival in Lima , the shocking news came that the Auca Indians (now called Waorani) of Ecuador had killed five missionary men. We felt grief for the men's families. The men were members of other missions, but we wondered what we would encounter in the tribes of Peru. Would we face martyrdom?

To facilitate our learning the Spanish language, Irma and I moved in with a Peruvian family, consisting of a father and his two unmarried daughters, Mechi, nickname for Mercedes, and Teri, nickname for Teresa. My two years of Spanish in high school helped me greatly, but Irma knew no Spanish, so it was more difficult for her. Besides living in a Peruvian home, we also studied the Spanish language and culture at Brown's Language School for three months, along with six other SIL members and two Methodist missionaries. On February 13, Mr. Brown, his wife, and baby came over to the Group House to visit during *Carnavales*, or Lent. He threw water and powder all over us, as was the custom of that holiday in Lima. Then we did the same to him. Mr. Brown, as head of the language school, spoke seven languages: six European languages and Quechua, the language of the descendents of the Incas. Mr. Brown arranged for us to take a trip down the coast of Peru to see the temples to the sun god and moon goddess of pre-Incan Pachacamac culture. They were large buildings, but men had previously tried to go into the rooms under the sun temple and died due to a poison in the air. Later, others entered with gas masks. In the sand surrounding the temple to the sun god were cloth, hair, and bones, remains of mummies. It was said that the bones were of virgins sacrificed to the sun god.

A long parade for the Lent holiday was held the next day. We followed Mechi and Teri, pushing our way through great mobs of people. The floats were beautiful, including one representing the many Chinese people in Lima. We were frightened that we would be lost in the crowd, besides being soaked with water and powder. Exhausted, we arrived back home at 11:30 p.m.

Our home stay and language study lasted until the end of March. On March 28, we awoke at five o'clock, had breakfast, and nine of us SIL people went to the Lima airport. We boarded a two-propeller airplane with Swiss pilot and flew over the stupendous Andes Mountains on a very cloudy day. Even the treeless soil and rocks took on various colors. The snow-covered mountains were extremely high, the highest being twenty-two thousand feet. Flying at such an altitude required that we hold oxygen tubes to our noses since the plane did not have any other oxygen. We flew over the forest-covered foothills of the Andes, then on over the level vast expanse of rain forest. We arrived in mid-morning at the small city (at that time) of Pucallpa, having a population of only a few thousand, on the Ucayali River. Stepping out of the plane, the dusty, hot and humid tropical air hit us. We rode in a truck out to the SIL base located on the west bank of Lake Yarinacocha, a twelve-mile long ox-bow lake. The base was like a small town. The streets were unpaved, dusty in dry season and muddy in wet season, the only two seasons in the rain forest. Near the lakefront was the radio shack, where the radio operator kept in touch with planes flying over the jungle and with SIL people in far-away tribes. The dining room, girls' dorm, the single men's house, and a scattering of private homes were in Yarinacocha, which meant "Palm Lake". The school for K-12 children was located on a small hill, and near the entrance to the base was the clinic with a doctor and nurses to minister to both base personnel and tribal people from the surrounding area. Most of the buildings had aluminum roofing and screened-in windows with no glass. The hanger and airstrip were at the north end of the base with a few one-engine planes with pontoons moored on the bank of the lake.

*Eight Years in the Amazon Headwaters*

Yarinacocha (Palm Lake) base of SIL/WBT

    The lake had a swimming ramp, but swimming was only allowed at certain times when many people would be in the water due to the danger from piranhas, boas, sting rays, and caiman, a South American type alligator. All these respected the area when many humans were swimming and making a lot of noise. But when a lone man went in swimming in the early morning, he was stung badly by a stingray, though he did survive. A nine-foot boa had swallowed a six-foot caiman just a few months before we arrived at Yarinacocha. Farther down the lake, a domestic cow which became bogged down in the lake was eaten completely by the piranhas. Even though the base had much appearance of being a busy, civilized small town, there were tropical dangers in this rain forest location.

    Vonnie Schreurs from Sheboygan, Wisconsin, and I moved to the girls' dorm. At that time Vonnie was corresponding with an SIL young man who later proposed marriage to her. She left Peru and joined him in marriage, after which they went to work in a tribe in Papua New Guinea. They had two little girls and worked there learning the language and preparing to translate. But one day a mountain exploded, burying their house and the whole family, something hard to understand, but which was in God's plan for their lives.

*Background and Preparations*

My first assignment was to be a helper to some other linguists. On March 30, 1956, I began typing stencils to mimeograph the Machiguenga Gospel of Mark. That tribal language has many extremely long words, but I worked my way slowly through to complete that assignment on April 12. Then I typed the Gospel of Mark in the Amuesha language, another real challenge that was eventually completed.

# PART II:
# SHAPRA-CANDOSHI TRIBE

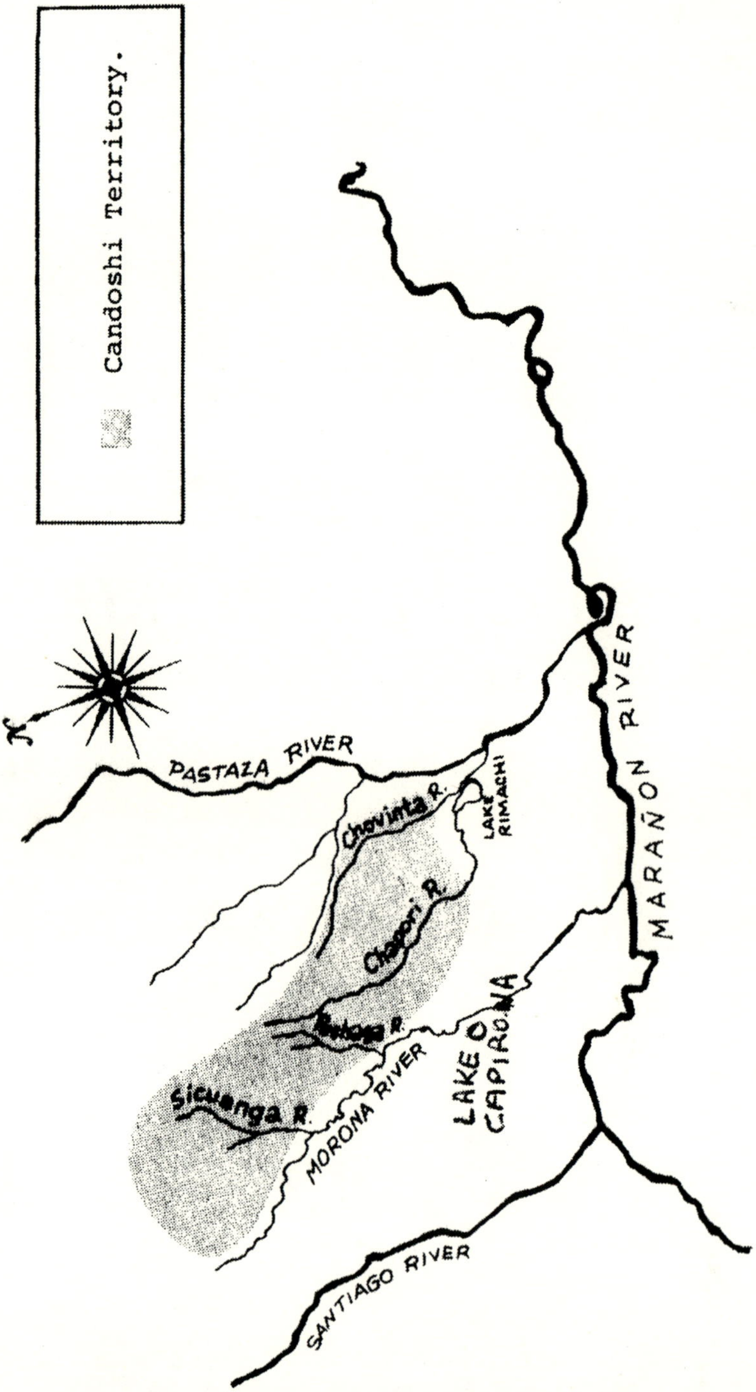
Candoshi Territory.
PASTAZA RIVER
MARAÑON RIVER
Chovinta R.
LAKE RIMACHI
Chapori R.
Sicuanga R.
MORONA RIVER
LAKE CAPIRONA
SANTIAGO RIVER

# *CHAPTER 3: FIRST SHAPRA TRIBAL EXPERIENCE*

After completing my typing of the Gospel of Mark in Amuesha, I was given a temporary assignment to go to the Shapra area of the Candoshi tribe with Lorrie Anderson (Loretta Doris). Her partner Doris Cox, accompanied by Mary Beth Hinson, was on assignment to another area of the tribe.

Loretta (Lorrie) Doris Anderson, partner
in the Shapra area of the Candoshi tribe

*Eight Years in the Amazon Headwaters*

Lorrie and Doris had been assigned as Bible translators to the Shapras. Their first task was to become immersed in the language and culture. They settled with a family group of Shapras on the Pushaga River, a tributary of the larger Morona River. Chief Tariri, a strong leader and a respected war chief, called himself "Chief of Seven Rivers." He had earned his title by having killed many enemies. He had their shrunken heads to prove it, though his prowess was well known. Lorrie and Dorrie later heard about their shrinking the heads of their enemies, but Tariri kept them hidden from the girls, he admitted later. "I didn't want you to be afraid."

Chief Tariri of the Shapras

*Shapra-Candoshi Tribe*

The Shapras were completely monolingual, speaking only their own mother tongue. The girls learned the difficult language slowly, but became very fluent after a while since they lived with the people and heard it continually. They wrote down everything they could, and practiced speaking it all the time.

The Shapras told them that if they had been men they would have been killed, but since they were just women they said, "What harm can they do? They're probably just looking for husbands." Shortly after they arrived, both Lorrie and Doris contracted a deadly form of malaria (falciparum) and were so weak they could hardly get out of bed. Lorrie had the further complication of black water fever, which is often fatal. They had a radio receiver, but the transmitter had been inadvertently left in the plane, so they had no way to contact the base. They slowly recovered after being at death's door. God healed them. They resumed their language study.

In 1952, Rachel Saint was assigned for a time to the Shapras with Lorrie. Rachel, with the help of Lorrie as interpreter, told stories to the children, and Tariri's crippled son Tsirimpo was especially touched. Rachel also, with Lorrie's help, talked with Chief Tariri and urged him to receive Jesus Christ as his Savior from sin. The chief listened with great interest. Lorrie spent each evening with Chief Tariri (the only time he had free) translating stories of the life of Christ from the Gospels. Each day following, as Tariri and the men worked together, he told them the story they had translated the night before. He was witnessing even before he knew the Lord himself. He appeared to be the only Shapra who understood the Gospel clearly, but he was not ready to commit himself to Christ. He was counting the cost. Should he give up all the teachings of the ancestors, the incantations to the spirits, and most of all the revenge killings? He would be risking his life if he gave up his position of leading his men to go on raids to the enemies. What should he do?

At the end of that year, Rachel proceeded to her assignment in Ecuador, and Lorrie went on furlough. Doris Cox, back from her furlough, went out to the tribe accompanied by Mary Beth. As soon as they arrived, before they could eat their lunch or change their muddy shoes, the people said, "Tell us about Jesus." Doris took out the typed copies of the Bible stories Lorrie had left with her. Included in them were the crucifixion and resurrection stories in Shapra.

Doris was able to talk with Chief Tariri in depth and realized he was close to believing. One day as he returned from hunting, Doris urged him to turn to Christ. He said, "Wait until I take a bath, I'm all dirty from the woods, and there is monkey blood on my skirt." She said, "No, do it right now. Don't wait." Doris sat down with Chief Tariri and explained again the way of salvation. He acknowledged that he believed that Jesus had died on the cross to cleanse his 'dirty heart'. So on that day of September 9, 1953, Doris Cox had the privilege of leading Chief Tariri to Christ. A proud headhunter, revered by his tribal brothers, cast all caution aside and chose to follow Christ. His life was changed. He said he no longer wanted to go kill the men who sought his life, because he knew God wanted him to love his enemies.

The chief wanted to teach his wife Irina and childen, brother and other tribe members to know Jesus as their Savior. He was an untiring witness. Shortly after, his son Tsirimpo went and brought Tariri's young half brother (also around twelve years old) to be dealt with, and receive Christ. Over the years the chief led all of his ten children to become Christians, most of them while small.

Later some enemies of Chief Tariri's arrived at his clearing and shot him point blank. The bullet pierced his lung about a quarter inch from his heart. Bleeding, frothing at the mouth, he managed to escape to a neighbor's house. They sent a runner upriver to the closest Huambisa village, and they informed their linguist, David Beasley, who radioed Yarinacocha base the news of Tariri's plight. Doris was at the base working on Candoshi language grammar problems, and Lorrie was out with Jeanne Grover and the Aguarunas. A plane was sent in answer to the chief's cry for help. Nurse Mary Beth Hinson went along to accompany Chief Tariri back to the base clinic, where the doctors cared for him and nursed him back to health. The chief and his extended family fled downriver to Lake Capirona, putting a good distance between themselves and their enemies who attacked him and killed his brother-in-law. It was to this new downriver location, off the large Morona River, that I was assigned to go with Lorrie.

On May 24, 1956, Lorrie and I loaded our duffle bags and supplies into the Catalina, a large amphibious plane which we called "the Cat." With much excitement and anticipation, I said goodbyes and looked forward to working in this unknown tribe. At 8:25 a.m. we took off from Lake Yarinacocha. As we flew along, the sun gave us a beautiful spectacle, the flier's cross. The shadow of the plane moved along below, reflected on the clouds and completely encircled by a huge double rainbow, resplendent in color. I thought of the rainbow as God's sign to Noah as protection from destruction by a flood again. Personally, I considered it as a sign of God's protection on our trip and later in the Shapra area of the Candoshi tribe.

Below stretched the rain forest as far as we could see. The green-carpeted foothills of the Andes Mountains were visible to the west. Flying to the Marañon River, we had followed the winding Ucayali River, then crossed overland. Where the Ucayali and Marañon Rivers met farther northeast, they formed the mighty Amazon River. By late morning, our Catalina plane landed on the Marañon at Angamos, a plantation and gasoline supply. The river was about a half-mile wide there. Pilot Leo Lance came flying in the small Aeronca one-engine float plane and also landed there at Angamos. The pilots unloaded our duffel bags and supplies from the Cat and put them into the smaller plane. We stepped up into the Aeronca, said our goodbyes to the Cat's pilots, and at 12:45 p.m. left for Shapraland. Flying along the Marañon, a short while later we turned north and followed the Morona River until we landed on the river. The Shapras were lined up on the bank to greet us. Chief Tariri was gone, so other tribal men took our cargo by canoe to the cluster of palm thatched-roof huts while we walked overland along trails lined with exotic tropical flowers, plants, and trees. As I approached the houses of the Shapra Indians on Lake Capirona, my excitement turned to dismay and my heart sank as I viewed my new home for the next three months: no walls, no floor, and no privacy for personal duties. We had just a ten by twelve-foot earthen floor covered by thatched roof held up by four poles and a pile of containers of Lorrie's belongings in the middle of the dirt floor.

Our home for three months with the Shapras

Pilot Leo Lance came with the second load of our supplies, then flew away, returning to Yarinacocha base. We were alone with the Shapras in the forest. We set about putting our living quarters in order. Our one piece of furniture was a small table. Our "chairs" were tin cracker boxes about two feet high. For beds, small logs were put down and covered with palm bark, on which we put our huff-and-puff inflated air mattresses and sleeping bags. My sleeping bag was filled with seven pounds of kapok, warm for the cool rain forest nights. After a light supper, we had a prayer meeting in Shapra language with the chief's half-brother Shiniki, of which I understood nothing. Then we went to bed exhausted just a few yards from the lake filled with anacondas and caimans.

The next morning we were up at 6:30 a.m. and called the base by radio to tell them we had arrived safely. Later in the morning, pilot Leo Lance flew in on the Aeronca plane with the rest of our supplies, then left. When I met Chief Tariri, he couldn't pronounce Lila so he named me Warakosha in the Shapra language. Lorrie's name was Monchanki and Doris' name was Mbawachi. Then the chief and Lorrie talked a good part of the day about what had happened while we were gone. He said that he had almost killed a man, which he had vowed not to do since becoming a Christian. He also told Lorrie that when his son was sick, he went to a shaman (a witchdoctor) to see if the shaman could cure him.

# CHAPTER 4: FOOD AND COOKING IN THE SHAPRA TRIBE

Since Chief Tariri and his group had fled down to the new location from up on the Pushaga River when some enemies there tried to kill him, they had only new gardens which were not producing yet. The lack of vegetables was supplemented with lots of fish from the lake. Now and then, they would make a quick trip up to the old gardens to get some bananas, plantains, and the starchy root manioc. Lorrie and I took turns cooking and washing dishes for a whole week at a time. I had a hard time adjusting to cooking on a log fire in the rain forest, but finally began to gain skill at the new task. Many days we had fish three times a day for our protein. Once I cooked a recipe of fish, onions, and cheese in the pressure cooker. As I mastered more fish recipes, I prepared fish chowder and even had a side dish of manioc French fries. Eventually, we ate partridge meat and other kinds of birds.

Some days we started the day with oatmeal, canned peaches, and coffee. Eggs and biscuits were sometimes prepared for breakfast, making the biscuits from scratch. Another day we had bacon and eggs for breakfast, a real treat. The bacon had come from the base on a flight. For lunch we once had squash, *chonta* (palm heart), and fish, all native foods. One day for dessert I baked a blueberry pie in an ovenette which is set over a kerosene burner turned low. Though the blueberries were from a can, the pie was delicious. One lunch consisted of canned sauerkraut, sausage, and canned apples. We had brought with us dried vegetables such as cabbage and carrots as well as powdered potatoes. The dried vegetables, soaked in water and cooked, all tasted alike.

One afternoon the chief brought in three monkeys which he had killed. The Shapras had singed all the hair off over the fire, making a black, hairless body, which was disemboweled, then boiled for a long time. They gave us some of the boiled monkey meat, but it was as tough as shoe leather. At a later date, when we were given raw monkey meat, we put it in our pressure cooker on the kerosene burner for over an hour and the meat was nice and tender—delicious. The monkey soup we made later was also good.

One Sunday dinner we ate South American partridge meat, mashed dried potatoes, gravy, and chocolate cake made from scratch. But on Monday we went native and had exotic large cooked ants and palm heart larvae. The ants tasted like peanuts. The palm heart larvae, developed in the heart of fallen palm trees, were clean since they had never touched the ground. About the size of a thumb, they were very fatty, but became somewhat crispy on the outside when roasted over the wood fire. They could also be cooked in a skillet, but we preferred them roasted.

# *CHAPTER 5: CONTINUING LIFE IN THE SHAPRA TRIBE*

We organized our hut, putting a crude rack above our beds and arranging our belongings. A short-wave radio kept contact with the base. But one day the wind blew down the tree to which our aerial was attached. The Shapra men put the wire back up, hooking it to another tree and the problem was solved. In the afternoons, we found a good place for privacy in bathing. We paddled the canoe to a spot out of sight of the huts and bathed in the canoe. The lake was off limits for bathing because there were stingrays, anacondas, piranhas, and caiman inhabiting the lake. Every time I leaned over the side of the canoe with my head in the water to wash my hair, I feared that an anaconda would grab my head and pull me under. But I trusted the Lord to take care of me.

On Sunday, we had a study of Bible verses in the Shapra language. I played my accordion which was not new to them since Rachel Saint had her accordion with her while on a short term assignment to the Shapra tribe a couple of years previously. Some of the Shapra men had invited Jesus to come into their lives, including Chief Tariri in 1953, but it was hard for them to break the cycle of revenge killings. They knew that Jesus wanted them to love their enemies, especially those upriver who had killed Tariri's brother-in-law and attempted to kill him.

On Monday, we again rearranged our hut, but in the midst we learned that Ishtiko was sick with malaria and had to give her malaria medicine. She was older than her husband Tsowinki. Previously, she had borne only baby girls but killed them all at birth because Tsowinki wanted a son. Before she was last pregnant, Ishtiko had asked Jesus to come into her life so, even though her child was a girl, she welcomed her and did not kill her. That was the last child she conceived, so that little girl was precious to her parents, and greatly loved.

Besides the malaria, Ishtiko also developed bronchitis that night, causing her to groan and vomit all night. The next morning we talked with the medical doctor at the base and he prescribed medicine for her. Complicating matters, it was raining day and night. We took her temperature and pulse, gave her the medicines the doctor prescribed, and she improved. Even so, later in the week she also had rheumatism for which she was treated.

After the weather cleared up, we could see three monkeys swinging in the trees as well as pretty little red and black birds flitting from limb to limb. We could hear colorful parrots and the larger Blue and Yellow Macaws loudly giving their calls that echoed through the forest.

One morning our radio wouldn't transmit. We could hear Luke Tanner, the radio operator at the base, but he couldn't hear us. On this first tribal assignment, I felt very alone without communication with the outside world. Finally, the next day Lorrie was able to fix the radio. She gave orders for items the plane could bring and broadcast news from our area so people at the base could pray for us.

By that time, I was teaching different Shapra men and women to read their own language. I really enjoyed this aspect of my duties. I also had regular classes with five children, teaching them to read the Candoshi language since there was not yet a bilingual teacher.

On June 8, the Quechua shaman Makawachi, his wife Sara, and young child came to visit. His wife was ill, so Lorrie diagnosed her problem and gave her an injection. Makawachi cured people who had been bewitched, using boa constrictor oil and chanting to the anaconda spirits. Even so, he recognized that some illnesses, such as infections or parasites, require white man's medicine.

On Sunday, June 17, after breakfast we treated a few medical cases, then the two of us had Bible reading and prayer in English. After we finished, Tariri blew the cow's horn calling the people to come to worship God. I had made a couple of dresses for the little girls, so we dressed them in their new frocks, and they looked so pretty. There were about seventeen Shapras present for singing, praying, and discussing a Bible story. Just after they finished, Sara, wife of the Quechua witch doctor, arrived with her little girl. We visited with her in Spanish, sang some Spanish hymns, prayed for her, and read a Bible passage to her. At two o'clock she left and we prepared dinner of fish and palm heart (the inner part of the palm tree), a delicious menu.

One day Tariri's wife, Irina, painted my face with bright red paint from the *achiote* plant in the forest. Then Ishtiko put a heavy load of beads around my neck. They both said that this was how I would look pretty if I wanted to find a Shapra husband. The many beads would impress him that my father had much money and a Shapra man wanted that kind of father-in-law.

How to look pretty, to find a Shapra husband

After supper one evening, we turned on the engine and I played a Kiowa reel-to-reel music tape from Oklahoma. The Shapras really enjoyed the North American Indian music of that tribe, especially the drums. Later, I took one of the Kiowa tunes and, with Lorrie's help, wrote Shapra words to it telling that a person did not need to be afraid of the evil spirits outside a house at night because God is stronger than the spirits. The Shapras expressed a desire for the Kiowas to come to visit them since they enjoyed their music.

On June 20, I had a bad headache most of the day, but still taught the children for two hours in the morning. After lunch I typed up a few recipes and poems, then went for my bath with the chief's daughter Mayanchi since Lorrie was working on the language with the chief. One never goes anywhere alone there. We did not undress totally to bathe, but washed under our dresses while sitting in the canoe. No slacks, only dresses almost to the ankles, are worn in the tribe. That alone was suitable for women according to tribal custom. After bathing, I washed a few clothes in the lake water. Returning to the hut, it was time to prepare supper, eat, and wash dishes. Afterward, we had prayer for the Shapra people. Still having a bad headache, I went to bed at 8:30 p.m. The next day my headache was gone, for which I was thankful.

Shapra worker Alex came to make separate tables for study, radio, and work. He dug holes in the soil that was our floor, placing the four poles firmly in the ground, then made the frame and the tabletop for each table. After my personal Bible reading in English, I taught little Mama to read for a while. She was a small, physically-challenged girl, whose growth had been stunted by tuberculosis of the spine. She had a hump on her back as a result. She was a sweet and loving Christian. Then lunchtime came and we ate squash, *chonta* (palm heart), and fish, all native foods.

Sitting at a new table to talk on the radio

The thatched roof had been leaking on my bed, so Tsowinki, Ishtiko's husband, was repairing the roof to stop the leak. Meanwhile,

*Eight Years in the Amazon Headwaters*

the men discovered a large poisonous snake down by the water and proceeded to kill it.

One day, Luke, the base radio operator, couldn't hear us but we could hear him. He said we should take down the aerial and check it. We followed his orders, solving the problem, and we finally made a good radio contact. I had a radio schedule with Irma, my future partner, who told me family news of my brothers and sisters. It was great to hear news from home.

Saturday and Sunday, June twenty-three and twenty-four, were rainy, dark days. The ground was wet and soggy. We took care of some medical cases after breakfast, then I polished my shoes and read my Bible. Tonsillitis began to give me pain, with headache and sore throat. Also, I had fourteen infected mosquito bites in that week. I spent the rest of Saturday in bed and then felt better. On Sunday when the Shapras were singing, they didn't all sing on the same notes together; it sounded like rounds in three parts. The culture pattern is not to have set words but to make up one's own words as you go along. Chief Tariri preferred this way of singing. If he didn't know the words he made up his own.

All the Shapra adults left the next day for the Pushaga River to get food from their gardens, leaving seven children with us overnight. The children, safe with us, went to sleep that night without fears or tears. With no walls and a constant humid breeze off the lake, my tonsils were overworked and inflamed. I continually had a swollen, sore throat. Because of the tonsillitis, I cut down my teaching schedule to just two of the older children, Powanchi and Mariwara.

The lake became very high from all the rains. We could hear the caiman grunting just a few yards from us in the lake at night. We knew that God would answer our prayers to keep us safe. On Wednesday after breakfast, I had a long talk with the doctor in Lima, the capital city, about my tonsillitis. After leaving the tribe, I would go to Lima to have my tonsils taken out. Meanwhile, the doctor prescribed medicine for me that would be brought out by plane. Later the plane came from the Yarinacocha base, circled, and landed, bringing the medicine and mail to us from the States and the base. It was always encouraging to hear from home.

After taking the medicine, my tonsillitis was better so I again taught all the children in the morning, the two teen-agers in the afternoon, and adult Shiniki after supper. It was necessary to teach the people to read in order that they might be able to read the New Testament after it was translated. While I was teaching reading, Lorrie gathered much ancestral history from an elderly man named Simu as consultant.

The next day after breakfast, the Quechua people who spoke some Spanish, Makawachi the witch doctor, his wife Sara, and their son, came to see us. Their son was very ill, white as a sheet and wheezing. The Shapras were afraid that it was contagious, so they kept their distance from him. We treated the boy, then sold a medical syringe to Sara and some aspirins to Makawachi to use in his business of healing people. After they left, I held my classes the remainder of the day.

On Sunday, July first, we had a two-hour radio contact with Lorrie's regular partner, Doris Cox, and nurse Mary Beth Hinson, who were at another Candoshi location. The Candoshis of the two areas talked with each other excitedly on the radio. While we were having radio contact, two Peruvian soldiers came. They wanted the Shapras to take a borrowed canoe back to its owner, which they consented to do. After the soldiers left, we finally had breakfast, a short devotional time in English, followed by a Shapra time of singing and Bible story. The Indians raved over the song which Lorrie and I wrote to the tune of a Kiowa melody.

On my last full day with the Shapras on this trip, I realized I had learned quite a bit of the Shapra language, and all my students had progressed in their reading skills of their own language. Lorrie had asked the women to hand sew Shapra skirts and blouses for each of us at our arrival. My skirt was a blue wraparound skirt down to my ankles. The long-sleeved blouse was cotton cloth with red flowers on white background and it hung loose down to my waist. This was our last day to wear the Shapra garb. In the evening we celebrated with popcorn and candy for all.

After breakfast on the day I left, I finished packing my duffel bag with my three dresses and remaining belongings. I was glad to be leaving this place of vicious gnats that even bit us on our legs under our dresses. We wore long sleeves, which helped keep them away, but the gnats still bit us on our faces and hands. One day we counted fifty bites in one square inch on Lorrie's arm.

The radio advised us that the plane would soon be on the Morona River. We left Lake Capirona, with all its memories, in the chief's large dugout canoe paddled by a Shapra man. The current was swift and we had to dodge tree trunks along the way. We arrived at the lake's outlet to the river just as the plane landed on the Morona River. We said goodbyes to our Shapra friends, who were like family to us, then boarded the little pontoon plane for the flight over the winding rivers with thick, tropical rain forest on their banks. I went to the Aguaruna tribe to the west, described in Part III, until the end of the year.

After my Aguaruna experience, I returned to Yarinacocha base for a short while, then flew to Lima to have my tonsils out. My surgeon was a British, German, and Spanish doctor who earned his doctorate in Germany. His nurse was a German woman who spoke Spanish. The doctor had me sit on a chair, then tied a blindfold over my eyes. He placed a pan in my lap, and gave me an injection to keep the saliva from flowing, drying up my mouth. He gave me a local anesthetic, then set to work cutting out my tonsils as I sat there with my mouth open. When the surgery was over, he removed the blindfold. There in the pan on my lap were the bloody cotton swabs while the tonsils were in a pan on a nearby shelf. I healed quickly and had no problems such as the nausea my sister Lois experienced in Houston when her tonsils were removed under sedation. There would be no more trouble with tonsillitis.

# CHAPTER 6: SECOND TRIP TO THE SHAPRA TRIBE

A little after noon on Wednesday, January 2, 1957, Lorrie Anderson and I took off with pilot Don Weber and co-pilot Gene Smith in a small single-engine plane. The pilot made a message drop to a Piro tribal village on the banks of the Ucayali River, then we crossed overland in our pontoon plane, which, of course, could not land in the forest. During each overland crossing, the people at the base were alerted by phone to pray for us. There were only a few tiny streams in this tropical forest-covered jungle. After crossing safely, we finally arrived to the great Marañon River and made our way to the plantation named Angamos, where the pilots could refuel the plane. We arrived at Angamos at 3:30 p.m. to spend the night before going on to Lake Capirona where we had been before. Only part of our luggage arrived with us. We discovered that we had Lorrie's air mattress but not mine. The two of us spent a restless night trying to sleep on one air mattress. It was a cool night, and we also had only one sleeping bag opened out like a blanket. We were glad when morning came.

Lorrie, the pilots, and I ate breakfast, packed our belongings, and were off the water early. It was a cloudy morning and the rivers were very low. After flying three-quarters of an hour, we landed upriver on the Morona where we waited for about an hour at the entrance of the stream leading to Lake Capirona where the Shapras lived. The stream to the lake was pretty dry, making it necessary for us to walk back to the lake over the trail for about an hour. This time our equipment and belongings were piled in the middle of the floor of our welcome new house on the other side of the lake. At this location, the bank was a little higher so we would not be surrounded by water as we were previously. We were grateful for the new house, but it needed some organization. By that evening we had restored some order. We made up the one bed again with a single air mattress and only one sleeping bag zipped open. The plane would bring the rest of our luggage the next day.

After another night with very little sleep, we were again on the radio talking to Luke at the base to help the pilots of the larger plane, the single propeller Norseman, which was going to Nazaret in Aguaruna tribe territory. We relayed the weather conditions to the plane since it was rainy. When we weren't on the radio, we spent time organizing the house. Lorrie was asking the Shapras about what had happened while we were gone. After I made supper and washed the dishes, we sang praise to God with the Indians.

On Saturday, we talked frequently on the radio. Pilot Don Weber arrived from Aguaruna country and brought my precious air mattress, sleeping bag, and other belongings. The pilot and co-pilot Bart left their plane on the Morona River and walked by trail to our clearing, arriving at 7 p.m. in the soaking rain. We had supper together, then I played my accordion. The pilots sang for the Shapras and told of how they came to know Jesus Christ as their Savior, translated into their language by Lorrie. Bart also did some sleight of hand tricks to entertain the Indians. After a pleasant evening, the pilots walked over to the chief's house to sleep. We were ecstatic since they had brought my sleeping equipment, giving us each a good night's sleep.

We were again on the radio on Sunday seeking weather reports until the heavy rain finally stopped. We said goodbye to pilots Don and Bart who flew back to their families at the base. The Shapras gathered to sing praises accompanied by my accordion and to study translated Scripture verses. After dinner, Shapra men Antoni, Tanchima, and Shiniki came to visit for a while. Then Irina, the chief's wife, talked with Lorrie about two hours revealing rumors that the Pushaga River people wanted to kill off our downriver group. The men discussed this topic also until everyone decided that we would trust in God to keep us safe.

On Monday, Lorrie talked with Antoni, Shiniki, and Tanchima again about the tribal situation. I studied Shapra language lessons to improve my conversing, then wrote a letter in Spanish for the chief to give to Makawachi about paying debts.

The next day I opened the school materials and flannelgraph figures for Bible lessons to organize them. Lorrie would write out the Shapra translation for each Bible story and I would read them to the children while she met with the adults. The rainy season continued with a hard rain most of the afternoon. Fortunately, the day before a group of Shapra men dug a drainage ditch around our house to keep the rainwater out.

The chief had a reading lesson before breakfast the next morning and made good progress. During breakfast, three Peruvian soldiers and one flirty officer came to visit. We talked with them in Spanish for a while about our work with the Shapras. After they left, I taught the school children in our hut.

By the end of the week, I was in a regular schedule of teaching the chief before breakfast. As on my previous trip, I taught the children after breakfast. Teaching them was somewhat trying. The children had never been to formal school before, and, therefore, were unruly and undisciplined. However, they were learning to read and proud of it. The fact that I knew little of their language was also frustrating. But, after all, this was just the second day of classes with them! In the afternoon I tutored teen-agers Tsirimpo and Shiniki who were also making good progress.

After teaching, I cleaned out and labeled the large metal Field brand cracker and cookie tins. With their tight lids and silicon inside they were perfect for storing items like cameras and films to keep out the humidity. Even though it was January, after supper we celebrated a belated Christmas with the children, Chief Tariri, Irina, Ishtiko and her husband Tsowinki who was Tariri's half-brother. Kool-aid and popcorn were our refreshments for everyone, after which we played a game. Our gifts for them were whistles, balloons, fishhooks, and dolls. The Shapras were very appreciative of the gifts.

As time went on, the chief's reading ability improved greatly. The children's reading also improved, although it was frustrating when they told each other the answers to questions. They acted up, particularly the chief's son Oroshpa, who was a lively child. I didn't have enough of their language to discipline them. A young man from the tribe would be chosen later and trained to be a bilingual school teacher in the Candoshi and Spanish languages. My teaching was only introductory. Shapra primers needed to be made for teaching more advanced reading. We had only two simple primers, but I worked preparing a new primer for printing.

One day when the kerosene stove could not be lighted, we thought that the kerosene had become contaminated. We cleaned the stove and put new wicks in it. Lo and behold, it worked—the kerosene was fine and we thanked the Lord for simple blessings.

Our beds were made right on the palm bark floor, just a few inches from the ground. One night I was awakened in the middle of the night with a sensation that something was jumping on my sleeping bag. The mosquito net was tucked all around the edges to keep out animals and insects. I reached for my flashlight that was lying just above my head. Shining the light brightly, I saw a cute little field mouse that had nuzzled his way onto my bed. Sleepily, I just lifted the mosquito net and shooed him out, then went back to sleep. Eventually, the Shapra men made us new beds, so much better than sleeping on the floor.

Two men of our Shapra neighborhood, Alex and Tanchima, went with the chief to Tsowinki's house and began arguing about making a canoe. All the men except the chief drank the fermented manioc, called *masato* in Spanish, and got drunk. In that state, they began to argue. Lorrie tried to calm them down, but all except the chief were beyond reason. Lorrie took Tsowinki's gun away from him so that no one would get hurt. After a while the three men left to go downriver to visit the *mestizos* at their settlement. There they would have to speak Spanish—difficult for them in their condition. They didn't know much Spanish anyway, and could hardly communicate when sober.

Irina, the chief's wife, began hemorrhaging, possibly having a miscarriage. In order to stay with his wife in her condition, the chief sent the boys Shiniki, Tsirimpo, and Shutka to tell Tanchima that he couldn't help him make a canoe. It was not characteristic of a Shapra man to stay with his wife instead of going with the men, but as a Christian the chief had special love for Irina. The boys came back later saying the men didn't believe that Irina was ill. We were pleased that the chief had stayed behind with his ill wife, exhibiting Christian values. That night we had prayer with her, and her health improved.

One day two Peruvian taxidermists who worked for the United States Museum of Natural History came. The chief decided to go to the Pushaga River with them even though he had seen an effigy of sloth smeared with red *achiote* hanging there, which was a warning that he was a marked man and in danger of being killed by his upriver enemies. He trusted in God to keep them from being attacked by the upriver enemies again.

While the chief was gone, the school children, including his own, heard a loud "boom" and said it was a falling star and that it was a sign that their father would be killed. We had prayer for the chief's safety and resumed school. The next day Tariri came back saying he had a good trip. The taxidermists stayed at Pushaga upriver, but were afraid for their lives. That evening we heard a loud noise down at the canoe port and we all went to see what it was. The Indians said it was spirits, but we thought it must have been some animal or snake which made the canoes hit one another and echo.

On one Sunday, there was a good group of Shapra visitors for the singing and Bible lesson. I put the pictures on the flannelgraph board while Lorrie told the Bible story. The people seemed to understand and follow the story well. Afterward we prayed for the people.

On the first day of March, Chief Tariri arrived at our house hot and tired, half-mad, half-joyful to tell us that the governor of the area would be coming soon. We cleaned up our house and the chief's to prepare for the governor's arrival. He came in the afternoon with Soplin, a trader in the area. Soplin brought guns and other things to sell, but also gave Tariri a list of his debts, a total of $5,000 in all. This was a terrible jolt to the chief, for he did not know how he could pay that debt. The traders always greatly overcharged natives for mundane items and kept them eternally in debt.

After the governor and trader left we went swimming in the new canoe port which had been cleared of trees. The weather had become sunny and beautiful. Swimming had always been forbidden and would be again in a few days. Little did we know why.

# CHAPTER 7: THE ANACONDA ATTACK

One morning in March, I finished teaching the children about 9:30 a.m. Lorrie had finished washing the dishes and treating the sick, and finally found time to have her devotions. Since Chief Tariri and his brother-in-law were fixing the thatched roof above our bedroom, there was no quiet place in the house. Tariri's wife, Irina, suggested that she go down to the lake shore and sit in a canoe. It was a lovely, balmy day, and it seemed like a good idea.

After she had gone, I went down to the outhouse which the men had finally constructed for us. Just as I stood up to leave, I saw a long green snake on the wall at the entrance. It had been just a few inches from my head when I entered. I stooped down and ducked out, then called Chief Tariri. By the time we returned to the outhouse, the snake was gone, but the chief said that it was deadly. I would have died that night if that poisonous snake had bitten me.

The men went back to work, and I was beginning my new task when I heard four blood-curdling screams from down by the water where Lorrie was. Could the children be doing something to scare her? I ran to the bank where the path goes down to the old canoe port which was not cleared of brush and trees like the new port.

Lorrie was standing on the bank with a frightened look on her face and said in a quivering voice, "He got me!"

"What?" I asked.

"*Isaria!*" she cried.

"What is that?" I asked.

"A boa," she answered.

Then I realized that blood was streaming down her arm, and I saw blood stains on her blouse and skirt. Fear gripped me when I realized that an anaconda had attacked her and bitten her many times, once on the chest and several times on her left arm as he tried to get a good grip in order to wrap around her and squeeze her to death.

It had been a perfectly beautiful day to have devotions at the lakeside—quiet, cool and inspiring. Lorrie had sat in a large, sturdy canoe which, unlike others, had a wooden seat. Her back was resting on a tree along the bank. The lake was high and muddy since the Morona River had overflowed into the lake, but this didn't distract from the beauty of the spot. Lorrie sang all four verses of the hymn "Beneath the Cross of Jesus." Then she read her Bible, a chapter on Elijah, and did a Bible study on that portion. She wrote in the margin, "Sometimes we have to have a time of trouble in order to know who God really is, and what He can do." She never dreamed how apropos that would prove to be. She then began going over her prayer list of loved ones at home, everyone at Yarinacocha base, and the Shapras, most of whom did not know the Lord at that time. As well as praying for the unbelievers, she also prayed for the new believers, and for them and Chief Tariri as they dealt with their enemies. She was sitting quietly with her notebook before her, glancing occasionally at it to see the next names for whom to pray.

Lorrie, her eyes closed, had just finished pleading with the Lord for the soul of old Chief Shotka from the Siquanga, Chief Tariri's enemy who had come down to kill him. Suddenly she felt a heavy weight thrown against her chest, and severe pain in her breast, and she screamed. She opened her eyes to see an enormous anaconda coiled in the water beside the canoe ready to strike again since he could not get a good grip the first time. He had come over the side of the canoe to attack her body. It let go and stood eye to eye with her, standing three or four feet out of the water. His head was even with hers, its piercing beady, yellow eyes fixed on her, his mouth opened wide, with rows of tiny teeth and two fang-like teeth, one on each side.

Quick as a flash of lightning, she saw the anaconda slide back into the water, then lunge at her once again. Lorrie instinctively threw up her left arm in defense. Again and again he struck in a slashing attack, biting into her arm and hand. She struggled furiously to get away, but she was no match for the powerful anaconda. The hungry monster surged from the water again, arching his back above her head, ready to wrap his coils around her in a death-dealing embrace. After three attempts to gain a firm grasp, and a powerful attempt to coil about Lorrie, the anaconda inexplicably relaxed his grip on Lorrie's arm and slid back into the water and disappeared.

"There's only one answer," Lorrie says. "I believe God said, 'That's it. That's enough.'" Fortunately, the canoe had been large enough not to tip over in the midst of the struggle, and tied so that it didn't drift from shore. Lorrie climbed out of the canoe, bloody and shaken.

We walked up the hill to our house and into our bedroom. Lorrie sat down and I began making preparations for cleansing her wounds. Irina, the chief's wife, came over, and, with one look at all the blood, she began to cry and wail. That made Lorrie cry, then all the children began to cry. I got a lump in my throat and my eyes smarted, but it was my responsibility to clean the wounds so fought back the tears. Lorrie was seated by the medicine cabinet. I put an empty pan in her lap and began cleaning her arm and hand. There were about five or six rows of teeth marks on her left arm and a deeper gash in her right hand. All these were cleaned, as well as her breast wounds, where there were twenty-one teeth marks, which she counted later. I put antibiotic medicine on all of them along with bandages.

As I was taking care of the wounds, we heard a flurry of activity over across the way at the chief's house. We didn't know what that was about, but we found out later that Makawachi's father, an old Quechua witch doctor whom we had never met, had just come with his daughter-in-law, and they were asking for Monchanki (Lorrie). The Indians simply told them that she was busy and could not be disturbed. The woman, Sara, ignored them and marched over to our house and onto the porch. Just as I was applying the antibiotic, some children pulled aside the unbleached muslin curtain which served as our door. Thinking it was Shapra children, I scolded, *"Papcha!"* Instead, it was strange children who turned out to be Sara's children, as she suddenly appeared. She said, "Oh, do you want me to get my husband to call the anaconda back?" We said, "No thanks," and she left with her father-in-law. We had no idea what that was about until Lorrie had returned after some time at the base.

With everything under control, I radioed the base and told the story. They asked if Lorrie wanted to return to the base, but she said no. As I was talking with the doctor about future treatment, the Indians saw a large anaconda crossing the lake. Amidst shouts of excitement, they raced to their canoes to go after it, only to come back disappointed since it got away.

That night the Indians set a trap for the anaconda. The men wanted to kill the anaconda to prevent further harm to other people and to revenge for Lorrie's attacks. The men tied a chicken to a tree where Lorrie's canoe had been tied. A large fishhook was tied to the chicken. Then the chicken was left there, and the men planned to rush to kill the anaconda when they would hear the chicken squawk. We went to bed thinking, "About the time we fall asleep, the boa will come."

After a while of deep sleep, we were awakened by the noise of a nearby jungle storm with lightning and thunder. Then I heard the chicken's squawk! One of the dogs, which had not been tied, was the first to the bank and was barking, startling the boa. Tariri and Antoni ran to kill the boa. Antoni slashed the tail of the sixteen foot snake diagonally with his machete as it lunged back into the water. It was an adult anaconda, long and black, the Indians said. They said it was as big around as the post that held up the roof. A year later the Shapras killed that anaconda which had the cut scar on it, so they got their revenge.

I had been reading about Satan's power in the life of missionary Fraser of Lisuland in Asia, and felt that Satan had been working much during this time out in the tribe. I also read how Jesus commissioned his disciples and gave them power over evil spirits and snakes. Truly God had snatched Lorrie from the clutches of death. The Shapras were very much in awe of the anaconda. The spirit of the anaconda was the most powerful in their pantheon of spirits. Chief Tariri said after the attack, "The spirit of the anaconda is very powerful, but God is greater." Lorrie felt that God had saved her from the attack to show that He is more powerful than the boa. She said that even strong Candoshi men had been killed by anacondas, and who was she to escape? It was by God's power.

It wasn't until they had gone back to the base, and Lorrie returned to the Shapra village, that they heard the rest of the story and learned what had gone on behind the scenes. Chief Tariri told Lorrie that after we had left, Makawachi, the young Quechua witch doctor, had come to visit him and bragged that he was the one who had sent the anaconda to kill Monchanki. Perhaps this Quechua shaman worshipped the anaconda. In any event, Makawachi evidently drank some kind of hallucinogen and went through his incantations. He chanted to the spirit of the anaconda and sent him to attack and kill Lorrie. Then when he felt he'd made contact, he sent his elderly father, also a witch doctor, and his wife to go and see if his purpose was accomplished. They must have been very surprised to find that Lorrie had indeed been viciously attacked by the anaconda, but was still alive.

Lorrie never told this part of the story for years. It was too weird. She believed it, but she didn't think anyone else would. Even most Christians back then, she thought, were not too aware of the power of our archenemy, Satan. After a number of years among the Shapras, Lorrie knew only too well how Satan worked. She believed that Makawachi had the ability to tap into Satan's power, and send that anaconda to kill her. The old witch doctor, Makawachi's father, and his daughter-in-law, would have had to leave their distant village an hour or two ahead in order to arrive at Tariri's village immediately after Lorrie was attacked.

The old witch doctor, Makawachi's father, had never come there before. He came that once, but never again. Nor did Lorrie ever see Makawachi and his wife again. Not long after that, Chief Tariri told her how the young witch doctor met his end. He had a horrible death. He was fishing, and, as was their custom, he bit the fish's head to stun it, so it would not jump out of the boat. It wiggled and slipped into his mouth and down into his throat. It was the kind of fish that has armor and spikes. There was no way he could pull it out, and he suffocated.

Several years later, Lorrie had a singles' party at her house at Yarinacocha base over five hundred miles away from the Shapra village. The guests were North Americans, tribe and base workers. One of the visitors to the base, who happened to be studying zoology, went into the bathroom. He called out, "Lorrie, I didn't know you kept one of these in your bathroom." She thought maybe it was a frog, or even a scorpion, which might occasionally be found there, and went to see. Lo and behold, there was an anaconda in the toilet bowl. She thought, "I can't even escape them here at Yarinacocha base!" She said, "David, that's not nice to play a joke on me that way," thinking he had planted it there. However, when she saw the struggle he had to get it out, she knew he could not have stuffed it down there. It had entered the septic tank and followed the pipes into the bathroom stool. He had to pull and pull in order to get it out, and when he did, they could see that it was about six feet long, just a "baby". But the struggle was not over. Just as David got it out of the toilet bowl, it latched onto his thumb and sank its teeth into him. None of the other men was brave enough to rescue David from the boa, and certainly not the women, so Lorrie helped hold it until David could release his finger. He put it outside and let it go. A zoologist would never kill it. Someone said, "Where there is one boa, you will sooner or later find another," but fortunately none ever appeared again at Lorrie's house, though various poisonous snakes appeared in the yard from time to time.

# CHAPTER 8: LIFE AFTER THE ANACONDA ATTACK

For some time after the attack, Lorrie had nightmares about that event. On Saturday, March 9, Shapra men came to work on our house. They built palm tree bark walls to enclose the bedroom, storeroom, study, and visiting room. I was busy moving boxes and cans, as well as sweeping to clean up after the workmen. As I began sweeping, I picked up the broom, felt something swish against my hand, then saw a scorpion drop to the floor. I quickly stepped on and squashed it. Once again I was spared from pain.

The Shapras gathered to sing on Sunday, so I played my accordion to accompany their tunes and choruses. Lorrie read and explained some translated Scripture.

The men finished our rounded end of the roof very nicely on Monday. They also made a wall of palm tree bark to form a hall and fence-like walls in the schoolroom at the new rounded end of the house. Upon completion, I moved boxes and goods to straighten up the house in order to begin our reading classes again. Afterward, I lettered primers for teaching reading. Alex, with his family, and Antoni came to visit for a while in the afternoon, as well as Lucho, a *mestizo* from nearby.

The next day we had invited all of the parents to come to an open house at the school. The children performed a simple program, with each child reading a page of the primer, then all reciting together and singing songs they had learned. The parents were proud of their children. After the program, the children played a simplified baseball game using a stick for a bat and a soft rubber ball.

I read in Luke 17, "Does he thank the servant because he did what was commanded? So you also, when you have done all that is commanded you, say 'We are unworthy servants; we have only done what was our duty.'" I was feeling sorry for myself that I was working so hard, and yet I only did what was my duty to do. I prayed, "Lord, help me. Make me a better servant." The Gospel of Luke, chapter 18, verse 1 reads "They ought always to pray and not

*Shapra-Candoshi Tribe*

to lose heart." This related to my reading of a book on prayer. The Lord always hears and answers, so we must keep on praying in faith. One of the main questions I was concerned about was what tribe and partner would I have to work with after the yearly conference at the base in December. My prayer was, "Lord, I now trust these decisions into your hands and thank you for your answer. Keep me from speculating on the future and prepare me for whatever it holds."

Tsirimpo, the chief's oldest son, went hunting. At dark he had not returned so was assumed to be lost in the jungle. Everyone was anxious about him. Finally, the chief heard him blow on his gun barrel, from which he calculated his direction and distance and went to get him. On another occasion, in the afternoon Tsirimpo, with Tariri's oldest daughter Mayanchi and their younger brother Oroshpa, went across the lake in a large canoe to go hunting on shore. They were gone for a long time and, as it started to get dark around six o'clock, they still had not returned. After darkness had fallen, we feared something had happened to them, and their parents were worried. Lorrie and I climbed into a canoe to look for them. Now we realize that we were crazy to go off in a canoe in the dark. It was an eerie, foggy night, and as we aimed our flashlight ahead, we could see the shining red eyes of caimans, a little smaller than North American alligators, lying in wait in the water ahead. Lorrie was paddling the canoe while I lit the way. Suddenly, we saw a canoe ahead of us on the lake. All was quiet as we approached it. Suddenly we gasped. Little brother Oroshpa was alone, sleeping in the canoe that had floated away from shore. An anaconda could have grabbed him and swallowed him whole! We woke him and questioned him about his two older siblings. He only knew that they were hunting somewhere on shore. We called repeatedly until the two finally found their way out of the darkness to the shore. They had lost their bearings when the canoe had floated away, and were relieved to hear us and find their way to the lake to be taken home.

Chief Tariri, his son Oroshpa, Tsowinki, and Ishtiko went upriver to the Pushaga River in the taxidermist's launch to get the rest of Lorrie's belongings which had been left there. Everyone had fled so quickly when the chief was shot by his enemies upriver that there was only time to pick up a few things to bring down to Lake Capirona. The taxidermist came back downriver with the chief. We invited him over for breakfast and discussed the rain forest and tribal life for an hour and a half. We had a tablecloth on the table with a vase of flowers as we ate a breakfast of pancakes. We had not forgotten how the outside world lived.

Each time that I was assigned to a tribe, I was given a native language assignment to turn in to the linguistics office at the base. I worked on my Candoshi language assignment which was to record a story from the chief, write out the story, and translate it into English with Lorrie's help. I typed out the paper to complete the job. The plane was supposed to come the next day to take us back to Yarinacocha base, so after finishing my language assignment, I worked on household packing and my own packing. We put shelves up in the storeroom, labeling and listing the supplies to be left behind. Two Shapra families came to bid us farewell. Also the trader, Soplin, and other *mestizos* came to tell us goodbye. After visiting with them, I cooked the noon and evening meals, weighed my luggage for the airplane, and visited with other Shapras.

The next day the Norseman airplane left the base bound for Nazaret in Aguaruna country, but it had motor trouble at the town of Yurimaguas, delaying them for some hours to repair it. I wrote some letters, read, and cooked while Lorrie packed since we were both going back to the base for our yearly conference. It was a few days until the Norseman plane came for us. We told all the Shapras, who had come to be like family, goodbye and climbed into the plane. The Norseman flew us to Angamos on the Marañon River where we met the larger Catalina plane which flew us on to Yurimaguas. There we picked up four other SIL workers from two other tribes, and flew on to Yarinacocha base to end our Shapra adventures.

# PART III: THE AGUARUNA TRIBE

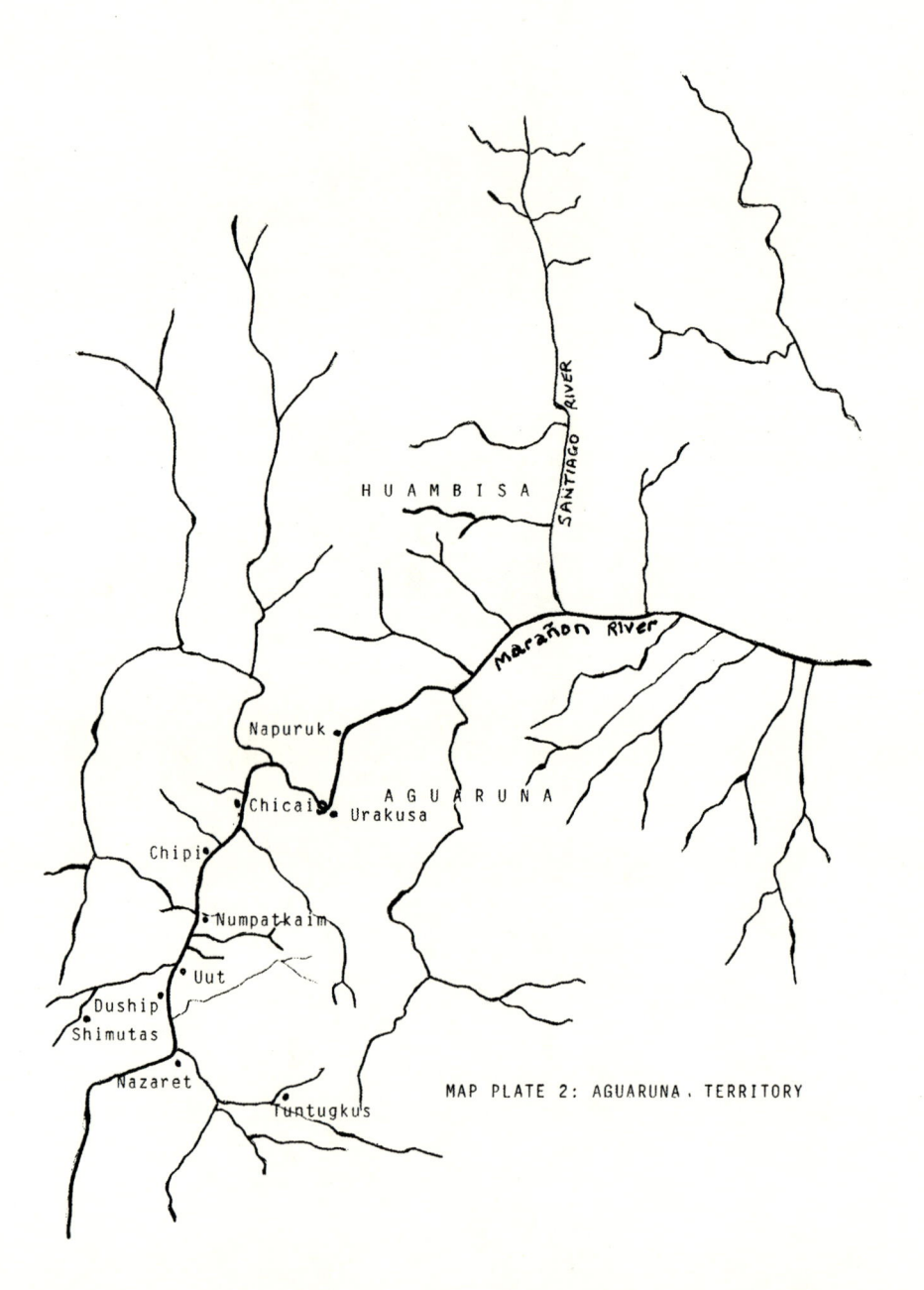

MAP PLATE 2: AGUARUNA TERRITORY

# CHAPTER 9: FIRST TRIP TO THE AGUARUNA TRIBE

Many people have heard of the Jivaro headshrinkers in South America, but not so many have heard of the Aguaruna tribe. The Jivaro tribe in Ecuador and the Aguaruna tribe in northwest Peru are both members of the Jivaro language family. Their ancestors used to be headhunters who would kill their enemies, cut off their heads, and put them through a process to remove the skull. The skin was shrunk with the face and hair intact until the shrunken head was about the size of a baseball. Even at that small size, the face could be recognizable. Peruvian law did not allow this practice when I went there in late summer of 1956, and the Aguaruna people knew this well, especially along the main Marañon River. However, back in the hills, up in the headwaters of the smaller streams, some few men continued this practice. The purpose of collecting shrunken heads to hang on the man's belt was to gain spirit power from men who had special strengths and knowledge, especially from warriors who had been very active in revenge killing.

On the flight to the Aguaruna tribe, Irma Schaal (my future partner) and I were in the larger Norseman plane over the flat, lush rain forest south of the Candoshis. At the Marañon River we turned west, flying over the left side of the river until we came to the first, main 5000-foot ridge of the foothills of the Andes Mountains. There were ominous, dark clouds behind the high ridge as we approached it about level with the top of the ridge. Since the storm ahead looked so bad, the pilot and co-pilot decided to turn to the left. Just as we turned, a down draft from the storm hit us and started pushing us downward. I could see the altimeter winding down from 5,000 to 4,000 to 3,000, and I had to look up to see the forest below us. Irma covered her eyes and said, "I can't look!" The pilot put on the gas so he could get power to pull up, thus speeding downward to 2,000 and 1,000 feet. Could he pull up in time? Our hearts pounded and we prayed that we would be able to land on the river. Finally, the pilot was able to pull up the nose of the plane, just missing the tops of the

*Eight Years in the Amazon Headwaters*

trees, and we slid into the river. We all breathed a sigh of relief. By that time a torrential rain was pouring. Across the wide river was a Peruvian army station that we hoped would be a haven for us. The pilot had to taxi clear across the river facing a tremendously strong current, but eventually made it to the other side. A soldier on the riverbank in the pelting rain grabbed the rope which the pilot threw to him as he shouted, "That was a great landing, Captain!" We all agreed that it was great and miraculous.

While the pilot and co-pilot tied down the plane securely, Irma and I braved the rain without raincoats or umbrellas. Our clothes were soaked quickly as we ran to the nearest building for shelter. We felt very conspicuous under the eyes of the many soldiers in uniform, especially since we were North American women with wet clothing clinging to our bodies. Since it was just past noon, we were escorted to the dining room of the base where we were seated. We were served a good, hot Peruvian meal. By the time we finished eating and chatting in Spanish with a few of the soldiers, the sun had come out through the white clouds. Around two-thirty the pilot said, "It's time to go!" Our clothes had dried pretty well by that time, so we felt more comfortable walking back to the plane under the eyes of all the soldiers. We girls, the pilot, and co-pilot boarded the Norseman, really a cargo plane that had only two seats on one side for us behind the pilots' seats.

After taking off, we first gained altitude before crossing the first mountain chain which was the boundary line into mountainous country and the foothills of the Andes Mountains. These were covered with rain forest, but had a cooler temperature than the lowland areas. At that first mountain chain, the Marañon River squeezed through a narrow gorge with the mountains on either side. Below was the *Pongo de Manserichi*, a series of huge whirlpools caused by monstrous rocks at the bottom as the river narrowed to pass between the mountains. The land to the west had mountain peaks from 5,000 to 8,000 feet high. Flying above the fleecy, white clouds, now and then we could peek between the clouds to see our river route below. As time passed, we could see the sun sinking toward the clouds on the horizon. But fear began to grip us when the clouds grew thicker as we approached the ridge of mountains along

*The Aguaruna Tribe*

the edge of the valley where Nazaret, our Aguaruna destination, was located. We could not see the gorge where the river cut through the mountain chain into the valley of Nazaret. We could not see the mountain chain because of the heavy clouds. We prayed for an opening in the clouds below us, as the sun was setting behind the clouds. Suddenly, the pilot found an opening in the clouds revealing the top of the ridge bordering the valley. He crossed above the ridge, then dove below the clouds in the valley, landing safely on the river. We had seen two miracles in one day! The pilots could not leave because of the great downpour that lasted two days. They slept in the plane to be sure it was safe on the river. Finally, they were cleared to leave.

The Norseman landing on the Marañon River at Nazaret

We were met at the river by linguist Mildred Larson (Millie) from Minnesota and nurse Jeanne Grover from the state of Washington. These two young, single women had begun their work among the Aguarunas in 1954, just two years before Irma and I arrived. Actually, Nazarene missionary Roger Winans was a pioneer missionary to the Aguarunas from 1932 to 1948. He showed love for the Indians and began to work at Yama Yakat, downriver from Nazaret. Sadly, first one wife died, then after he remarried, a second wife died due to the difficult life in Peru. Later, Nazarene missionaries Elvin Douglass and his wife Jane took the Winans' place. They worked at Yama Yakat for nine years, Mr. Douglass having experience as a lab technician as well as in missionary gospel work. But the Nazarene missionaries did not have the linguistic and anthropological training needed to do the Bible translation which Millie Larson was prepared to do. Irma and I had come to help Millie and Jeanne. Irma would travel downriver with Jeanne, checking the seven bilingual schools; I would stay at Nazaret with Millie to take Jeanne's place doing medical work and checking some on the Nazaret bilingual school. Millie would finish translating a summary Bible story book into Aguaruna language and also work on writing up the grammar of the language, which was required before actual Bible translation could begin.

Although I had been trained in boot camp to administer tropical medicines, I was further trained by Jeanne during these three weeks before she left on her downriver trip with Irma. There were first aid cases, but the number of cases of malaria was tremendous. Practically every other tropical disease was well represented, especially intestinal parasites, yaws, pinta, and leishmaniasis. The latter three required special injections. During my stay I averaged ten patients each day, with around 250-300 treatments per month. This number is small in contrast with the large number of cases in surrounding areas. Considering the fact that there were approximately twenty thousand Aguarunas scattered among the foothills and the disease rate was so high, the medical needs of the tribe as a whole were barely being touched. Besides nurse Jeanne, what other sources of medical help were available? The Peruvian government had appointed a doctor to serve the tribe, but he was in the town of Bellavista, a two-day hike over the mountains, a difficult trip for a sick person to make. Also, not too far from Nazaret, Mr. Elvin Douglass, the Nazarene missionary and excellent lab technician, was located. However, he was busy with medical work, schools, and evangelistic work at his location.

Millie had prepared lessons for Irma and me to learn the Aguaruna language. During those three weeks the four of us were

*The Aguaruna Tribe*

together, Irma and I were busy studying lessons about greetings, conversation about family members, numbers, medical terms, body parts, buying and selling, and other basic terms. The house in which we were staying was much larger than the ones in which I stayed in the Candoshi tribe. The huge palm-thatched roof was rounded on each end. On one end was the entrance on the ground level with a circular cane pole wall. Next to the rounded wall were benches for visitors to sit. The rest of the house had a raised palm bark floor about two feet off the ground. It had a kitchen area, bedroom for Jeanne and Millie, store room, medical room, and table area which served as a desk for Millie to work on the language at the one end of the living room. We had plenty of opportunities to practice the language since many Aguarunas came to visit or to receive medical attention, gathering in the circular room on ground level.

The large, Aguaruna-style house which was home in Nazaret

The Aguaruna lived in kin groups in oval-shaped houses on the tops of hills. The large palm leaf-thatched buildings with rounded ends had only one door at the men's end of the house. Walls were of vertical cane poles or palm bark placed one next to another so close that a mouse couldn't get through. The women and children occupied the other end of the house with no door. There they had their three-log fires for cooking, the three, large logs having one end meeting together forming the fire area, with the other ends spread widely apart in y-shape. Near the fire were shelves for cooking pots, some metal, bought from traders, and some ceramic. Hand-made, large, ceramic pots with a small end on the bottom to fit over the three-log fire were used to steam food. Water was put in the bottom, then sticks on which the food to be steamed was laid inside the pot. The top of the large pot was covered with pieces of banana leaf tightly tied so none of the steam could escape. That was their primitive pressure cooker. The fire would be made where the log ends met and after the ends of the logs were red-hot, the cooking pot would be set on. The main starch foods were manioc and plantains grown in their gardens. Wild animals hunted were mostly deer and wild hogs. Also, a few smaller animals were killed for eating. Papaya and palm heart, as well as a few other wild nuts and berries, were part of their diet. The men practiced slash and burn gardening, the men clearing the ground for gardens and the women weeding the gardens and harvesting the fruits and vegetables. Women went together in the morning, taking their small children to the garden area. One of the women took care of all the children while the others worked, except for babies who were kept inside the mother's hand-woven sarong-style dress to nurse.

The typical woman's dress was a large, one-piece, hand-woven cloth wound around the body and tied tightly over the right shoulder. If the woman had a baby, the infant would be inserted into the dress on the left side. An older woman past child-bearing age would often put a cluster of nuts inside her dress to increase the appearance of her breast. A woman might wear a safety pin on her dress as decoration, or one or more necklaces of seeds or beads. She might wear a short cluster of colorful feathers as earrings. In contrast to the men's fancy ornamentation, the women's decoration was quite simple.

*The Aguaruna Tribe*

Aguaruna women and girls' sarong-style dress

The men wore hand-woven skirts which reached from waist to knees, one piece of cloth wound around the body and doubled one side over the other in front, kept in place by a hand-woven belt. The men went shirtless for hard work or wore shirts bought from a Peruvian trader who would come by periodically on the river. To dress for a fiesta or special occasion, a man would wear a ponytail with special ponytail tie decorated with multi-colored feather clusters. Aguaruna women did not wear ponytails; it was a man's hairstyle. A man

*Eight Years in the Amazon Headwaters*

would also wear a crown decorated with colorful feathers, or even a crown of monkey tail fur. He would wear bandoliers which were chest adornments over both shoulders and crossing over his chest and back. The bandoliers were made of strung beads, nuts, and seeds. From his ears hung shimmering green iridescent beetle wing earrings down to his shoulders. Fiesta regalia also included a collar made of buttons, and beaded wrist-bands.

On our first Sunday morning, Alias Dantuchu gathered some people in our ground floor visiting room to sing some Aguaruna songs, and hear Alias teach a Bible lesson. Alias and his brother Daniel Dantuchu had attended a Nazarene Bible school on the coast which had classes only in Spanish. The boys did not know Spanish and those at the school did not know how to speak Aguaruna. Students who spoke a language other than Spanish were normally given Spanish names. When asked what their names were, Alias and Daniel told them "Dantuchu" in Aguaruna meaning "I don't have a name," since they had not been given a Spanish name yet. So their teachers put down "Dantuchu" as their last name. Later, Aguaruna students gave their father's name as their family name. Alias and Daniel Dantuchu both became Christian leaders in the Aguaruna tribe. Alias had been nicknamed "Boney Eyes" when, as a non-Christian, he had gone on a revenge killing trip, and killed the enemy's wife instead of the man who was his enemy. He had also married a widow and her daughter. The Nazarene missionaries had made him put away the widow from being his wife, citing an Old Testament law in the Bible that one should not marry both a mother and daughter. Alias had confessed his sins and made Christ the Lord of his life. The New Testament had not yet been translated into the Aguaruna language.

After the Aguaruna meeting, we girls sang hymns in English as I played the accordion. Also, that morning I was named *Dada* since there were no L's in Aguaruna. Later in the day we went on a tour of the area. We went to the house of Kunyach and his family, our nearest neighbors on the next hill. He was like a chief of the Nazaret area. Millie and Jeanne had nicknamed him "Father." After a short visit, we climbed the steep hill behind our house to see the bilingual schools where children were taught to read and write in Aguaruna,

*The Aguaruna Tribe*

then in Spanish. They were thatch-roofed buildings with earthen floors and cane pole walls.

A bilingual school at Nazaret with Peru's official shield and a large flag pole

From the school buildings, we tramped on through the mud to peek in a house where a fiesta was going on. The women were drunk on the alcoholic beverage *masato*, made from the manioc root which had been cooked, then chewed by the women and spit back into the pot. It looked like a pot of mashed potatoes. It was then allowed to ferment from three to five days, depending on how alcoholic one wanted it to be. It was then mixed with water for drinking. The women were dancing and jingling the beads, nuts, and shells which decorated their bodies. Young married women wore arm-bands decorated with shells that jingled, just as we wear wedding rings. We stayed only a few minutes, then carefully went back home down the slippery, almost perpendicular hillside.

Even this early in my stay, working with nurse Jeanne, I gave an injection and took some temperatures of babies. A baby was brought in which was skin and bone. We gave it some medicine and it revived. But we heard that the sick baby had died the next day, and the mother tried to hang herself. Aguaruna women seemed to have frequent cases of suicide or attempts at suicide. Sometimes it was from being mistreated by the husband. Another cause seemed to be when a close relative died and she wanted to die with him or her. One day a woman wailed all day because her brother had died. Grieving for him, she took the poison of the *barbasco* root and became very ill but, fortunately, did not die. Each day I gave two to five injections to people of all ages and observed Jeanne doing her medical work. I filed some of the medical cases, making me aware of some patients whom I would continue to treat after Jeanne was gone downriver.

Jeanne, Irma, and I went to visit "grandpa", whose daughter was ill. It was a nice little hike, taking a full hour on the muddy trail over hill and dale. Grandpa's thatched-roof house was walled in with cane poles. Inside were three beds, two fires, a table with metal dinner plates, and a bench. We visited a short time as Irma and I practiced using some of the Aguaruna sentences we had learned so far, mostly about our families.

Each morning I typed a while on an Aguaruna dictionary which Millie was preparing. One day while I was typing, an Aguaruna man came and tried to take away the baby of the woman who washed our clothes. Millie held the baby tightly and wouldn't let him have it. News came from downriver that Alias' brother Daniel Dantuchu, main teacher and leader at Chicais, was very sick. A teacher from another area also came in the evening with news and requests for help with teaching. The bilingual schools, with teaching in Aguaruna and Spanish, were just beginning to function, so there were many needs for help. This teacher was teaching for the first time, had forty students, and few books. There were two pupils to a book in some cases, and they had no writing books and no blackboard. We had much to do to get primers prepared and ready for use.

Aguaruna men prepared to go help teacher Daniel. As they prepared to leave, Jeanne came down with high fever and chills—the dreaded malaria. After Irma and I reviewed our language lessons, we took care of the twenty or so medical cases we had that day plus Jeanne. Neither Jeanne nor Millie had taken malaria prophylaxis to keep from getting the fevers because they had never had a problem with malaria before. I had been taking malaria prophylaxis when in Shapra territory, but quit when I arrived in Nazaret.

*The Aguaruna Tribe*

A recuperated Daniel arrived at Nazaret with his wife and two children who were all ill, as well as a woman with tuberculosis. I climbed the steep hill behind our house twice that day and again the next day to take care of them.

The Aguaruna men killed a tapir, also called a *sachavaca,* meaning "wild cow." This short-legged animal weighed up to two thousand pounds and is related to the rhinoceros. The meat was the closest we could get to beef. For supper we had tapir hamburgers, almost like home.

Jeanne had a patient who was named Jorge, son of our neighbor Kunyach. Since Jeanne had malaria, his care fell to me. We weren't sure what his physical problem was, but he had been losing weight and complained of pain in his abdomen. I gave him an enema and hoped that would help him. I was glad when, by the end of the week, Jeanne was well again.

In a few days, Jeanne was able to climb the hill, accompanied by Irma, to visit the bilingual schools as a practice run before going downriver to visit the other six bilingual school locations. The teachers from many tribes were paid by the government and would fly to Yarinacocha base or go by river or road to be trained from January through March by professors sent from Lima. This was the school year's summer vacation time used by bilingual teachers to move up to a higher grade in elementary school since most of these men had very little schooling before becoming teachers. Some of the men, such as David, Daniel, and Alias, had been trained by the Nazarenes in Chosica, a city on the Pacific coast. They had learned to read and write first in Spanish, though they originally spoke only Aguaruna. Some of these men read only word by word, and did not learn to read for meaning because they were learning in a new language. However, that was years before and they were older men now. A few of the younger men, such as David Kunyach, who learned to read Spanish first, did learn to read for meaning and became more fluent in Spanish. Students who learned to read first in their own language, Aguaruna, read for meaning and became good readers in both Aguaruna and Spanish.

Bilingual school teacher training buildings at Yarinacocha base

A group of Aguarunas, including Daniel who was still in Nazaret, gathered in our visiting room one Sunday. Millie began questioning him about the Aguaruna word for "God." They had a word *Apajui* for an Aguaruna god who lived in a cave way downriver at the entrance to Aguaruna land. This god had great power. Millie felt that description didn't quite fit that of our God, but she studied the word more and later decided that *Apajui* was the word to use for God with some teaching and explanations.

The following Friday, July 27, Nazaret became a beehive of activity. An airplane from the base arrived with pilot Leo Lance and co-pilot Paul Bartholomew, bringing a much-anticipated packet of mail with news from home in the United States. Also, the Nazarene missionaries, the Douglasses, came from downriver for a visit. We had a delicious chicken dinner while we all visited. We knew that our pleasant gathering was almost over when Jeanne and Irma excused themselves to pack for their trip by river to Chicais.

Saturday dawned a beautiful, sunny day for the plane to fly back to the base and for Jeanne and Irma to leave for downriver. We would miss them greatly. Mr. Douglass took blood smears on Jorge to see if we might find out what his physical problems were. Jorge required a lot of special care. My heart went out to him as I heard him crying out in pain at his house across the valley between our hills. With permission from his parents, we decided to have Jorge stay at our house. Millie moved her desk into a new room and we reorganized the clinic room. The next day Jorge moved into the clinic room where I could feed him soft foods, such as Jello, mashed manioc, and some canned foods. Slowly, with the soft foods, his pain lessened and he began to gain a little weight. Mr. Douglass had sent some medicine for treating him, which also seemed to work wonders. His pain was gone in about a week and he returned home to his family. Within a very short while, he was climbing the hill to attend the bilingual school. We praised the Lord for an answer to our prayers for Jorge. Unfortunately, several months after I left, with his tribal diet of roughage, his symptoms returned and he died.

On a Saturday afternoon, two Peruvian engineers came by our house. They were surveying the land and planning the route for the first road to cross through Aguaruna territory. That area of northwest Peru had been home to the twenty thousand Aguarunas for centuries as an area where there were no whites except men who came to this no-man's land to escape the law. The engineers talked with us in Spanish for a while, then gave Millie and me four pieces of chocolate candy. They went on their way to plot the route of the new road that would bring white settlers to Aguaruna land. Their land was already being sold in Lima along the route of the road. The government offered land papers to the Aguaruna communities which would build a bilingual school, pick a teacher to be trained, and take a census of their community. The people were illiterate, so in communities that had them, the current teacher would write down their names. The government would give a small portion of land for each person's name on the census list. With time, the cries, "We want to buy a teacher! We want our land papers!" echoed throughout the hills.

My new project was to type the twenty Aguaruna grammar lessons that Millie had prepared for Irma and me. I completed that project, and also finished Primer Number One bilingual school book and began setting up Primer Number Two.

The airplane returned with some supplies on August 29. Millie and I went over to the Marañon River to meet it, about a half-hour walk. We visited with the pilots only about ten minutes, giving them some baskets and artifacts the Indians had made to sell. When we arrived back home and ate lunch at two o'clock in the afternoon, we both had headaches. The next day Millie came down with malaria fever. Due to Millie's illness, I greeted all the visitors and took care of their needs, as well as prepared the meals and took care of Millie. I still had a headache and ached all over my body. On September first, I also came down with malaria. Chills came with the fever at 9 a.m., 3 p.m. and 9 p.m., typical of malaria. The fever went up to 101.8 and I was weak, dizzy, and nauseated. I had been taking prophylaxis to keep from getting malaria before coming to Nazaret, but not since I arrived except when Jeanne came down with it. There didn't seem to be many mosquitoes. I was infected, but had a lighter case than Jeanne or Millie due to the medicine I had been taking. Millie was almost completely recovered by the time I came down with it. In three days I was back to work. I treated twelve malaria cases and finished Primer Number Two diglot (two languages, Aguaruna and Spanish). It seemed that we were having an epidemic of malaria. A few years later the government sent men to spray DDT insecticide in houses all along the Marañon River and malaria was essentially wiped out.

We received the sad word that all of Jeanne's and Irma's supplies went to the bottom of the Marañon River on one of their dugout canoe trips. That greatly hindered their work, as they were going to give many of the teachers more books and supplies.

I continued learning the Aguaruna language with Alias as my teacher. As an assignment for my time in the tribe, he told me a folk tale that I wrote down in Aguaruna. I then asked him word for word what each word meant in Spanish. Finally, I wrote out a free translation in English. Meanwhile, Millie, as main translator for the Aguaruna language, was analyzing Aguaruna grammar and translating a Bible story book in preparation for later translating the New Testament. I did as many of the daily chores as possible to give Millie time for her more important work.

Aguaruna men began work on a clinic building for medical patients next to our house. They built all the wood framework of poles harvested from the rain forest. Each of four men tied palm fronds that had been bent in half, securing them with vines also from the rain forest. Each man on a different level tied the palm leaves all around the roof, one level lapping over the level underneath it on the upper edge. Then they put palm fronds over the peak of the roof. They tied vertical cane poles side by side with vines all around the framework of the house, placing the poles tightly together, leaving space for a door. When the building was finished, Aguaruna family members would stay in the clinic with their relatives who were ill.

Construction of Jeanne's new clinic building in Nazaret

Just as I had put the coffee water and a pan of eggs on the kerosene pressure burners for breakfast and was laying out silverware on the table, over the hill came Apatio's wife, bringing her little boy for a penicillin injection. It was 6:30 in the morning. Usually patients came at 7 a.m. so that I could take care of their needs right after breakfast. But this morning the patients were early. What was I to do? The syringes were all dirty and needed to be washed with detergent and boiled to sterilize them before an injection could be given. Should I finish preparing breakfast, eat, and then take care of the patients? No, I turned the breakfast fires low and went ahead cleaning the syringes. I was there to love, serve, and reveal Christ to the patient. I gave the injection, and resolved to boil the syringes and needles in the evenings to speed up giving injections to early patients.

All of the Aguaruna mothers nursed their babies. It was only natural since there were no cows or goats to give milk, and no stores at which to buy canned or bottled milk. These mothers sometimes nursed their children until they were four or five years old. The children grew up to be well behaved and generally there were no problems with delinquency. The mothers gave all their time and care to their children. They did not push them away and go about their business. The mother carried her baby inside the front of her sarong-style dress with a belt, so that the baby could nurse at any time. The children were secure in their mother's love.

Lieutenant-Governor Carrión came to visit at Nazaret. We had previously planned to go to the small island where we had a garden of fresh vegetables to harvest some for our meals. As a result, we missed seeing Mr. Carrión, which we regretted. But we had a treat for supper, fresh lettuce and squash pie.

One week there was a great fuss over the possible marriage of our Mitach, the woman who washed our clothes. A drunk man named August came down the hill, calling for her. For three days he drank and fumed and yelled because he was the father of her baby and wanted to marry her. Kakaja, by whom she had her first child, threatened to beat her up since the young man was her relative and she should not marry him. For refuge, she came to our house. The following night Kakaja was drinking heavily and followed through with his threat to beat Mitach. She screamed in terror as he hit her. Teacher David, our neighbor Kunyach's son, took up for her and had loud words with Kakaja. A woman had taken the baby away from Mitach during the day for protection, so Mitach again came to our house to stay. It was a dark, cloudy night with thunder rumbling in the distance. During the night Millie woke me to tell me that Mitach was gone. Afraid that she had gone to commit suicide, Millie went to look for her. She found Mitach sitting by the river; safe, but sad and concerned about what to do with her tempestuous life. The next day, after much consultation, the men met and decided Mitach would marry the young man who was the father of her baby. Then peace and quiet returned to Nazaret.

Besides having Mitach and her two children with us, there was a family of six people sleeping on the ground in the new clinic building. The grandmother of that family was very ill. The men returned to build more beds in the clinic house for the visitors. The four legs of each bed were stabilized by being planted in the earthen floor. Native beds were short and slanted, with the heads higher than the legs. A wood branch footrest was positioned over the low fire or coals beneath as the feet and lower legs rested on the footrest to keep warm on cold nights. Most nights were quite cool in the foothills of the Andes Mountains with an altitude of about four to eight thousand feet.

We had a grand reunion when Irma and Jeanne came back from their trip downriver on September 29. We caught up on the adventures they had while visiting all the bilingual schools. October first and second Irma and I packed, for the plane was coming to take us to the Yarinacocha base. I did medical work while nurse Jeanne got settled and wrote letters to go out on the plane. The plane left Yarinacocha, but was able to go only to the town of Yurimaguas in the expansive, flat rain forest. We were having fog, clouds, and a little rain. We could hear the plane's messages, but pilot Don Weber couldn't hear us to get the weather from Nazaret. The base could hear neither the plane nor us. By two o'clock in the afternoon, we had given up on the arrival of the plane, but suddenly we heard an engine and saw it coming over the mountains. The pass over the Marañon, their usual route for arrival, was clouded over. However, pilot Don Weber had opted for an alternate route. He arrived safely and decided to stay overnight in the plane. For relaxation during the evening, Don came to our house, and I played my accordion while Don played his harmonica.

Saturday dawned foggy and cloudy. We all watched the skies like hawks. By ten o'clock in the morning, we finally saw enough patches of blue sky to board our canoe for the trip over to the Marañon River where the plane was tied down. Irma and I could take only items weighing approximately five pounds each, which meant that I could take my little green cosmetic case and my basket-weave purse the Aguarunas had made. We had to leave practically all our belongings at Nazaret. The one-engine Aeronca was not running smoothly. Don said it should be "put out to pasture". We piled most of the weight in the front seat with me, and Irma sat in the back seat. The plane took off from the river and was circling to get altitude to fly out of the valley. One of the magnetos, part of the generator in the engine, was not working well. We had some tense moments, not knowing if we would make it, but finally it began to work normally. The pass was clouded over, making it impossible to use as a route. Our pilot had to use all of his flying skills to gain enough altitude to fly over the mountain. Don was barely able to clear the top of the mountain. After clearing the summit, he followed the Marañon River that was visible on the other side of the pass. We flew east along the river over the mountains, then out over the flat rain forest. As we flew to our rest stop, we passed the mouth of the Morona River, up which the Shapras lived. We landed at Angamos to refuel. For lunch each of us had only a piece of cake made by Millie back at Nazaret. Back in the air, we followed the Marañon east, then turned south on the Huallaga River down to the town of Yurimaguas, where we landed on the water to refuel again. Brethren missionaries met us at the river to chat a while. Even though the sky looked very cloudy, we thought we would try to reach Yarinacocha base. After we took off, the pilot immediately became aware that the magneto was again malfunctioning, so we quickly returned to Yurimaguas.

Brethren missionaries, the Coenhovens and the Elliots, gave us a place to sleep for the night. Irma and I stayed with the Elliots. Bert Elliot was a brother to Jim Elliot who was murdered by the Waorani Indians in Ecuador in January of that year. The Elliots had just come back from Ecuador a month before. They told us about their trip while we ate a delicious dinner prepared for us. Afterward, we walked around the plaza of this small Peruvian city before returning to the Elliots' home to go to bed.

The next day we were fogged in, so we went to Sunday school and communion at the Brethren church with fellow believers. After the service, the sky was clearing so we took off immediately in the Aeronca. We followed the Huallaga River south to where it turns

*The Aguaruna Tribe*

west, then flew over the dangerous rain forest for half an hour. During that time there was no place to land since we were a float plane. If a plane went down, it would be difficult to find in the mass of tall trees. Arriving safely over the Ucayali River, we followed it for an hour and a half, arriving at Yarinacocha Lake before three o'clock. Our many friends welcomed us warmly, after which we went to the rooms prepared for us in the girls' dorm. Pilot Don Weber's wife, Annabelle, made waffles for our belated lunch. We were so happy to take a real shower after unpacking our belongings. Dinner was eaten in the base dining hall where we chatted with our friends. That evening everyone on the base gathered to hear Irma give a report about her trip down the Marañon River with Jeanne to check on the progress of the bilingual schools and to give medical treatment to those who needed it. I had come to love the Aguaruna people like family, as I had the Shapras, and was thankful for my exciting experiences with them.

# CHAPTER 10: SECOND TRIP TO THE AGUARUNA TRIBE

While Mildred Larson went home to the United States to work on her Master's degree at the University of Michigan at Ann Arbor, I returned to the Aguaruna tribe with nurse Jeanne Grover. We left Yarinacocha base in the Norseman airplane at midmorning with pilot Leo Lance and copilot Bob. Our goal was to follow the Ucayali, Huallaga, and Marañon Rivers again to Nazaret, six hundred miles northwest of Yarinacocha. Being told by radio that we were on the half-hour crossover of the rain forest from the Ucayali to the Huallaga River, people at Yarinacocha base were alerted by six long rings on the telephone. That was the call for important announcements throughout the base; in this case, to alert people to pray while our pontoon plane went over forest where there was no place to land on water. We made it safely across, followed the Huallaga to the Marañon, and then refueled at Angamos. After that brief pause, we flew on to Pinglo, the army post on the west side of Boya Pass through the first mountain chain. There we landed and transferred our goods to the larger Catalina plane. We flew on, following the twisting Marañon River. Jeanne and I arrived at Nazaret where we were to stay only a short while. We went to the house to unpack enough for the night. This meant blowing up our air mattresses, then laying out our sleeping bags. We fixed a light supper, washed the dishes, and went to bed. The pilots slept in the Catalina on the river.

Our job there was to gather and pack our belongings and school supplies for the seven bilingual schools. The next morning I washed all the dishes which had been dusty and dirty. In the afternoon, I continued to set up the house and unpack, while Jeanne talked with the Aguarunas and met their medical needs. June 7 was a special school day with a Flag Day program which we attended, followed by a barefoot soccer game. Jeanne talked with Kaikat, a prosperous Aguaruna man who lived across the Marañon River from Nazaret. He had led some Aguaruna expeditions to Lima to ask government leaders for goods, such as knives, machetes, shirts, and trousers. The Aguaruna men who went to Lima dressed in their finest colorful decorations: bead and seed bandoliers, long iridescent beetle-wing earrings, feathered ponytail ties, and bright-feathered crowns.

Kunyach, our nearest neighbor and leader of the area, killed a deer. To do so, the men drove the deer into the river, then paddled a canoe out into the river next to the deer. They shot the deer and pulled it from the water into the canoe. Back on shore, they skinned and cleaned it, cutting it up to divide among the different families represented. We were happy to receive a large piece of the meat, but a visitor named Tuyas was thrilled to get the intestines. We were the first white people Tuyas had ever seen. When he first arrived with his wife, she wanted to feel our white skin and was awed by it.

Teacher Segundo came upriver from Chicais and ordered many supplies for the four schools located there. The books and supplies were then ordered by radio to come on the next flight from Yarinacocha base.

A heavy rain in the afternoon gave us a good supply of clean rainwater that we caught on a plastic sheet guiding the water into the fifty-five gallon drum. This was our main source of clean water.

I visited teacher David Kunyach's class to observe his teaching methods. The class was nearly all boys and men, with only one or two girls attending. Since this was the first bilingual school in Nazaret, the elders felt it was important to allow a majority of males to attend school because they would have to deal with the traders. Adult males attended to learn to read and write at this first opportunity. The class was very orderly and well-taught. On another day I visited teacher Alias's reading class, pleased to see that the children read well. I also visited arithmetic and Spanish language classes. After class, the children cleared grass, while typical long-haired men wearing shirts and skirts cut down trees around the school to enlarge their soccer field.

After observing classes, I baked bread and rolls. We used an ovenette that we set over the pressure kerosene burner to bake our goods. We also had deer-burgers for our meal, using a meat grinder to prepare the venison.

My new project was to type the Aguaruna-Spanish medical book written by Jeanne. I set up different situations to illustrate chapters on the different diseases, then took photographs which would be presented to the base artist to copy for the medical book. Teacher David Kunyach was translating the medical book into Aguaruna from Spanish.

Alias sang an Aguaruna tune that I notated with the help of my accordion. We put Aguaruna words to the song telling of how God's Son Jesus had come to earth from heaven to die for our sins. The people enjoyed singing this new song.

A very ill, elderly man was brought to the clinic, but Jeanne could not help him, and he soon died. All the people came from the hill behind us, mourning and wailing. Their style of wailing sounded like a chorus sung in rounds, with one particular melody sung over and over. The people believed the man's sickness came from witchcraft. The dead man was carried away in a hammock suspended from a long, strong pole. Although a few died, most of Jeanne's patients recovered from their illnesses. She had as many as twenty-six patients in a day during our visit to the village.

# CHAPTER 11: THE TRIP DOWNRIVER ON A RAFT

The Aguaruna leaders decided that we should travel downriver on a rather large balsa raft since the load of books and school supplies would be too great for the dugout canoes. We packed for the long trip downriver, and I made bread and canned three pints of deer meat to take with us. People kept coming all day to tell us goodbye on that beautiful, sunny day. A Peruvian geologist and his helper came by on his way to explore for oil. He took movies of us at the bilingual school. After packing, we went to bed exhausted.

The next morning we were up at dawn and took baths at the house with just a pan of water each. More people came to tell us goodbye, to get last-minute medicine, or to buy trade goods. At seven o'clock the raft was carefully packed, and the time came to leave our large, comfortable Aguaruna-style house. Our rowers were five Nazaret teen-age schoolboys whose only means of steering the raft was to paddle as hard as they could.

Leaving the quiet valley rivers, we entered the swift and wide Marañon River. The bottom of the raft grated on rocks in the shallow valley rivers, but in the Marañon, there were just balsa logs and cane poles between us and the black, rapidly-moving depths of water. Our rafting proceeded well until we entered the north pass through the ridge surrounding the valley. In the pass, the water was rough and choppy. In our bobbing raft, the water looked as if it would splash through the logs and soak our load, but only a small amount seeped through. We cascaded through the turbulence to calm water, with two boys paddling to keep us in the middle of the river. A raft cannot be steered like a canoe and is carried along quickly by the current. As we came to a big bend in the river ahead, the strong current swept our raft close to a piece of land jutting out into the river on our left. Fearing that the raft would crash into the land, we prayed while the young men paddled with all their might. The raft missed the land by only a foot, but it was upright and our goods were safely on board. We breathed a sigh of relief and thanks to God.

Floating swiftly past the Nazarene mission at Yama Yakat, we moved quickly downstream to Duship where we landed. Teacher Jum and some school boys met us to accompany us to Shimutas. The hike over the rugged mountains was stimulating on that beautiful day. After walking a short way, we stopped to eat fruit and palm heart for lunch. After a short rest, we continued, climbing higher and higher along the trails until we reached the crest. One section of the descent was almost perpendicular. The men of the village had constructed a railing alongside the steep, descending trail which ended at a rushing stream. We crossed the stream in water up to our waists, walking with difficulty in the rapid current. Across the water was the village of Shimutas with its bilingual school. The village provided us an Aguaruna house with a dirt floor, a large building with typical rounded ends, and walls constructed of cane poles. All around the house, we could see eyes peeking between the poles, watching our every move, since we were the first white people in their village. They had built beds for us, longer than theirs, but with the head higher than the feet in their style. We unpacked our bedding, blew up our air mattresses, laid out our sleeping bags, and fixed a small meal. Exhaustion from our hike over the mountain guaranteed a good night's sleep.

Jeanne Grover in an Aguaruna style
house with earthen floor and cane pole walls

*The Aguaruna Tribe*

Sunday dawned a beautiful day and breakfast was delicious. We were visited by many people who wanted to see the white women who spoke Aguaruna language. Mostly school children and women gathered to sing Christian songs in Aguaruna and to hear a Bible story from the bilingual teacher. Afterward, a blind, twelve-year-old boy was brought to us. We could not do the miracle of giving him sight, but other people were treated for malaria and parasites. In payment for medicine, the people gave us eggs, bananas, plantain, manioc, and fish. The people were very friendly, some bringing us firewood and others bringing water from the river.

One day Jeanne was called away for most of the day to visit a sick woman. I spent all morning and some of the afternoon helping teacher Jum at the school. The people next door to us were all drinking fermented *masato* to excess and were singing loudly and dancing. This went on all night with a bright and beautiful full moon.

The next day I spent all morning at the bilingual school, helping the teacher to arrange his classes into groups and to keep all groups busy. Also, I tried to teach the children to run relays. I was helping Jum with his record books after dinner. The teachers had to make monthly reports and keep attendance records. The monthly reports were especially hard for them to do, so we gave them assistance. Later, while Jum and a *mestizo* visitor talked in Spanish, I went to take a bath and wash my hair in the swift river. My hair is naturally curly and I cut it myself, helping me to feel cool and neat even in the tropics.

As days passed, I saw class order and discipline improve at the school. The children were learning to read, first in their own Aguaruna language and then in Spanish. Working together with the teacher, we were making the school look better physically and function well. We counted books to see how many more should be ordered. The "desks" were four poles planted in the ground with a plywood sheet placed over the framework to form a table. The schoolboys built a shelf and lowered one of the tables which was too high for the children. A grandmother swept the floor for us with a short-handled, hand-made broom.

*Eight Years in the Amazon Headwaters*

    Jeanne asked if there was a lake in the area where an airplane could land. The men said there was a lake nearby and, after packing a few items, we followed them along a rugged trail to see the lake at a place called Kagkas. Leaving early in the morning with teacher Jum, his wife, and six schoolboys, we hiked up a towering, craggy mountain. Climbing the mountain, we could hear the Shimutas River far below as we made our way along a narrow path, only about a foot wide in places. At times we clung to the side of the mountain to avert a fall of two hundred feet or more. We reached the peak at 9:30 a.m. and began descending the other side of the mountain. We clung to roots and crawled over huge rocks to climb down the steep cliffs. When we reached the bottom, we followed a small riverbed. The trail was muddy from springs coming out of the rocks. Jum showed us a place where the trail bordered a steep, wet rock and said a man had fallen off there but didn't die. We stopped and ate our chicken for lunch about one o'clock. After a short rest, the upward climb began again. After an hour of hiking, we could view the whole Kagkas valley out before us. The Shimutas River was glistening in the sunlight and we could see the Kagkas River running into it. What a beautiful sight! We went down the ridge and had to cross the rushing Kagkas River. With no canoe or balsa raft in sight, the Indians pulled off their clothes and began ferrying our baggage across. They swam underwater with one arm extending above the water, holding the goods. Eventually, a man came with a balsa to ferry us across the river, just after we had worked up enough nerve to swim across in the swift current. We would soon arrive at the lake, the purpose for the rough trip. Since the Indians had said it was a large lake, Jeanne had envisioned the possibility of her and Millie living there, since the road would be built through Nazaret soon. We hacked our way through an unblazed trail to arrive at the lake, which, to our dismay, turned out to be a small, muddy frog pond. The Indians knew nothing about large lakes or airplanes and were unable to make such judgments. In our disappointment, we hiked back to camp, put up our jungle hammocks, and made supper, consisting of packaged chicken soup with crackers, canned pears, and coffee. Jeanne had been suffering terribly all day from a cold or allergy, sneezing and blowing her nose. Very tired and

*The Aguaruna Tribe*

disappointed, we went to bed about nine o'clock. However, I awoke during the night and could not sleep because my legs ached and my feet were higher than my head. I turned around to the other end of the hammock and slept well the rest of the night.

Next morning, a Sunday, we left camp at 8:20, hiking along a wide and smooth trail, higher and higher. After stopping to eat bananas, we began to climb in earnest, hanging onto each root, climbing straight up on hands and feet. Finally we were on our feet, walking again. We reached the top and walked along a ridge, often climbing over rocks and passing by huge boulders along the path. It was a cloudy day and very dim down in the forest. We gradually began to go down and seemed to be hanging on to the steep mountainside until we reached the bottom. We made one last, valiant struggle up a hillside to Yumau's house. Though it was a cool day, we were wringing wet with perspiration. While resting at Yumau's, I played with a baby parrot. We proceeded to the river by a spongy, moss-covered trail. Again, the boys pulled off their clothes and ferried our goods and bedding across. We joined hands and waded to the other side, almost swept off our feet by the current. Our clothes—and we—were wet to the hips. After walking along the ridge of a hill, we were soon home in Shimutas at 1:30 p.m., wet and tired. We took a quick bath in the river, then had a late dinner, just glad to be back.

There were always more tips to give teacher Jum about teaching at the bilingual school. We rearranged the seating, then had the students dictate words for spelling, giving both reading and spelling practice. I taught them a children's song in Spanish about baby chicks and helped Jum with his monthly school report. The classes seemed to be progressing well.

On a more mundane day, Jeanne and I washed a large pile of clothing at the river, then also washed our hair in the river. The schoolboys made clotheslines for us to hang up our clothes to dry. The people killed a chicken for our dinner—a treat after eating so much meat from wild animals.

We went fishing with the Indians one day immediately after our noon meal. They blocked off a section of the river and put poison *barbasco* in it to stun the fish so they could grab them and kill them.

The *barbasco* poison doesn't affect the people who eat the fish. After they put the *barbasco* in the water, we all felt under the rocks for fish. The people caught many fish and gave us a number of them. It rained heavily and our clothes were again soaked through. From all the hiking, my sneaker tore so I sewed it together.

One sick little boy named Katip ("mouse"), son of Dapi and Esamit, was brought to us. He had a puncture wound to his head, so Jeanne treated him for infection. He was having a hard time chewing when eating, so we feared that he was beginning to have tetanus infection. Unfortunately, we had no tetanus shots to give him. He was a cute, little, nine-year-old boy, one of the students in the bilingual school. We hated to leave sick, little Katip. However, it was time for us to leave Shimutas, so we packed our belongings and said *"Pujumata"* ("You stay!" or "Goodbye."), and hiked back to the main river.

Our journey continued down the Marañon River, this time in a dugout canoe accompanied by the clumsy raft. As we came near large whirlpools in the river, we would steer ashore, get out of the canoe, and walk on the shore past the danger. At times the boys carried all the cargo overland, then returned to walk on the bank pulling the empty canoe along through the shallow water. There are huge boulders at the bottom of the river, causing the relentless swirling of the water pushed by the strong current. Many Aguarunas have lost their lives in the whirlpools. The canoe would go to the bottom, then pop up to the top. Some lives were saved when individuals held onto a strong rope or vine tied to the front of the canoe. Holding on tightly, they surfaced with the canoe after spinning to the bottom.

We arrived at Uut where a bilingual school was taught by Shajian, a family man who had attended the Nazarene mission school. There he learned to speak Spanish fairly well and also learned to read and write Spanish. He had bilingual school teacher training and proved to be a good teacher. Shajian had prepared a house for us. We were in Uut to check Shajian's school records of attendance and grades, and to give him more supplies for his school. His wife Sakejat later went to Yarinacocha to attend the health promoter course. Shajian's son, Roman, was the first Aguaruna to attend university.

*The Aguaruna Tribe*

    Alias and I had composed Christian words to an Aguaruna tune and also written Aguaruna words to the tune of "I Have Decided to Follow Jesus." At each place we stopped, we taught these two songs. The people enjoyed singing the new songs. Jeanne was busy treating medical patients again. Our stay at that location was over all too soon, and we were packing and loading the large dugout canoe for our trip back upriver.

.

# *CHAPTER 12: BACK TO NAZARET*

On our return trip to Nazaret, we checked another school. Going upriver, at one point we heard wailing. Someone had died, and we finally learned that it was little boy Katip from Shimutas, who we feared had tetanus as a result of a puncture wound. His relatives decided to bring him over the mountain to the Marañon River to get more medicine for him from Jeanne. But on the way over, he died. The tetanus had given him lockjaw so that he could not eat and worsened with fever and other symptoms. In Aguaruna culture, a deceased person's name was not to be spoken after his death for a year or more. Since his name was Katip, or "mouse," they had to use another word when referring to the little animal. We felt sorry for his family, and that we couldn't help them. They took his body home for burial and, sad hearted, we went on our way upriver.

At one point we decided to walk on a sandy beach for about a mile while the Aguaruna men paddled and poled the canoe around a bend in the river. It was a hot, tropical day in northwest Peru not far from the Ecuador border and the equator. We left our rainproof panchos in the canoe, but Jeanne kept her waterproof cap on with matches in her pocket. All of a sudden we saw a dark cloud coming through the pass ahead. It was quickly upon us and we were soaked to the bone with a heavy tropical storm. Jeanne had placed the matches under her waterproof hat to keep them dry. The canoe finally caught up with us, but it was four o'clock and the sun would go down at six o'clock. We had to cross the swollen river to an island where the Aguaruna men knew there were lean-tos for some shelter. The men built fires with the little wood they could find. We used my poncho to cover each of us as we took turns taking off our dresses to dry them by our fire. We opened a few cans of food for our evening meal, then bedded down as best we could under the leaky lean-tos. Each time I woke during the night, I could hear the water rushing around the low island and had visions of the river coming up over us. But it did not, and we were safe all night.

Our canoe trip to Nazaret resumed the next day. At one location along the river, the men pointed out a canoe and said that it belonged to a Spanish-speaking man who had come to this area from the coast to escape from the law. Continuing on, we arrived home in Nazaret, safe and sound, at eleven o'clock in the morning. It was great to see our many friends there. By shortwave radio, we learned that the plane would be coming. I baked bread in the ovenette and also baked a cake to feed the pilots when they would arrive. Suddenly, we heard that the plane was almost there, and raced over to the Marañon River. Nazaret houses were along a smaller river which ran into the Marañon, the Tuntugkus. The plane landed and we greeted pilot Ralph Borthwick and co-pilot Porter Katerhenry. We especially looked forward to our letters from home in the United States. June fourth was the last we had heard from our families, and it was now July 24. Jeanne had many medical patients to treat now that the plane had brought new supplies of medicines. In the afternoon, our Aguaruna friend Tuyas came by to tell us that his baby had died. They had taken him to a shaman for healing while we were gone. Tuyas and other men accused a particular man of bewitching his child. They dragged the accused man off to Kaikat's house across the Marañon for judgment. The wife of Tuyas came to us grieving for her dead child. We comforted her and asked her to stay with us all night.

On Sunday we had fifty-five or sixty people in our visiting room to whom Alias taught a Bible story from the published book that Mildred had translated. The people also enjoyed singing songs that had been translated into Aguaruna. Afterward, about thirty Aguarunas came from Kaikat's area across the river. Also, five or six students came from Tuntugkus upstream. As in Nazaret, many of the nearly all-male students in the bilingual schools were teenage or grown men because that was their first opportunity to attend school. Later, in Chicais downriver, we knew of two male students who each had two wives and ten children. It was an Aguaruna cultural practice to have more than one wife. In the afternoon we went up the hill to watch a soccer game between Nazaret and Tuntugkus. The players were bare-footed since they owned no shoes. The Nazaret team won.

I continued to type the medical book which Jeanne had authored, worked on the layout, and prepared the index and flyleaf. Aguaruna Apatio and some boys went downriver for salt. We saw them off, taking two balsa rafts and a large canoe. One day just before noon, Payach brought a huge tapir leg that weighed thirty-one pounds. We ate one meal, then I cut up and canned seven pints of tapir meat.

Several friends at Yarinacocha base and I had a radio schedule. I talked with Irma, my future partner in the Cashibo-Cacataibo tribe, more than anyone else.

We woke up the next day to rain, thunder, and lightning. This was good to fill our rain barrel. After my devotions and breakfast, Walter, Vicki, and Meteg, children of our neighbor Kunyach, expressed concern about *iwanches* (spirits). They said someone must have gone to kill an enemy somewhere because neighbor Wapik's dog was bitten by a snake and died. They did not believe this would happen unless someone was bewitched and would die as a result.

Bilingual teacher Felipe came from his downriver village of Numpatkaim to visit us. He made a good impression on Jeanne. But when neighbor Kunyach came home and talked with Jeanne, we learned the awful truth that Felipe was guilty of sending schoolboys to harm someone. Felipe was sent to an Aguaruna jail. The Aguaruna men had gathered to discuss how they could punish wrongdoers, and decided to build jails in each location of the bilingual schools. With more vigor, I worked on translation into Spanish of the teachers' rules, including one about how they should live exemplary lives for their students.

One day we went with Misagkit, Kunyach's wife, to get palm heart and palm heart larvae. The larvae were considered a delicacy and were often a gift of love from a man to his pregnant wife, or just a gift to someone admired. Jeanne and Millie had been given palm heart larvae at times. To reach the fallen palm tree, we frequently walked through mud over our ankles on the swampy trail. The Indians dug larvae out of felled trees which had been lying on the ground about two months. There were many larvae, each about one and one-half inches to two inches long, the size of a thumb. They were very fatty, white in color, with a large brown head. The Aguarunas would pop them into their mouths raw, biting off and spitting out the head. They relished eating them. We also chopped the palm heart out of the fallen tree. After arriving home, we fried some palm heart larvae and roasted others over the three-log fire. The palm heart was made into a delicious salad.

Two motor boats went up the smaller Muchigis River which ran alongside Nazaret. Later, they returned, carrying road crew men and engineers who were scouting out a route for the first road to go through Aguaruna territory.

July 28, Peru's most popular holiday, celebrates independence from the Spanish. There was a two-week school holiday to observe winning the war for independence. August 12 was the first day of school after the holiday. In the bilingual schools, the students began to study Peru's history and pledge to the flag simply to have a sense that they were Peruvians, not just tribal people. They needed to have this background knowledge to prepare them for the invasion of white people into their territory when the road was completed.

After intensive work on the Aguaruna-Spanish bilingual medical book, David Kunyach, teacher son of our neighbor Kunyach, finished translating Jeanne's book into Aguaruna. Wampukai and Tomas were proofreading it in the afternoon. Working all day, I completed typing it, then pasted pages together to form a book.

Jeanne was treating many people for leishmaniasis. The disease started with the bite of an infected sand fly, usually on the leg, ankle, or foot, to produce a large, ulcerated sore at the site of the bite. It was best to begin the multiple, painful Repodral injections at an early stage. If the injections were not begun, the disease entered the blood stream, causing enlargement of the nose and destruction of the inside of the nose and back of the throat. The patient died due to the inability to swallow food. At that time, the injections were so painful that even grown men, who usually would not express emotions, would weep. Jeanne had a radio talk with Dr. Eichenberger and found that he did not want her to allow the Indians to give Repodral injections. She had already let Kaikat start fifteen men on a series. Leishmaniasis was almost at an epidemic level. Later, when the government men sprayed for malaria-infected mosquitoes, it appeared to kill off many of the leishmaniasis-infected sand flies as well.

After the leishmaniasis cases were under control, a fever began spreading through the village population. The fever temperatures were persistent and high, but it was not malaria. All ages of the population, from babies to adults, were infected, causing Jeanne to have many patients.

The Norseman, a large one-engine plane, came late in the afternoon on August 21, a Wednesday. We had been writing letters and packing items to send on the plane. Leo Lance and Jim Baptista were pilot and co-pilot. We prepared for them a special dinner of fried chicken and vegetables, topped off with cherry pie that we all enjoyed. We talked until midnight to catch up on all the news of the world that we missed while we were away from Western civilization. Then the pilots walked over to the airplane at the Marañon River to sleep and keep watch over the plane. The next day it rained all morning. Finally, the pilots took off after lunch. They took some of the baskets the Aguarunas had made to be sold in Yarinacocha or Pucallpa.

We listed all of the belongings of SIL/WBT members Ray and Alice Wakelin that were in our house at Nazaret. They had lived and worked among the Aguarunas before Jeanne and Millie arrived. Ray, a Canadian, had impaired health from working in this difficult place and had to return to Canada with his family. Life in the Aguaruna tribe was difficult.

Alias prepared a Bible lesson that he would give. On Sunday there were about sixty Aguarunas present. There was a lot of commotion with dogs barking, babies crying, people spitting over the wall (about five feet high), and people talking. Aguarunas did not believe in swallowing their saliva, so they always spit it out. They were masters of spitting over the edge of a floor or over a five-foot high wall. They believed that saliva was harmful for a person to swallow.

One morning, I took photographs of many of the people for their identity cards that the government required. Afterward, a baby was brought to us having a fever of 107.4 degrees which caused convulsions. We worked with the child all afternoon and evening to bring the fever down. We treated the child again the next morning, but to no avail, for the baby died. The mother, holding the dead baby inside her dress in the customary manner, began to wail the melodious, but sad, tune of grieving. She asked me to take a picture of her holding the baby as a remembrance, which I did. Relatives of other deceased people had asked me to take pictures of their loved ones so they could remember them. I had a reputation of being the one to take pictures of the dead. Never in my life did I have so many experiences dealing with the dead until I came to live with the Aguarunas.

Jeanne was called to go and examine a case of what they called measles. There was a very sick child on the beach. All the Indians were fearful, knowing that measles was a killing disease in their area. But it appeared to be an allergy. Nampag and many others ran away before they were sure what the disease was. Later, the ill boy was vomiting roundworms and had fever, so Jean treated him for both. In the afternoon, a man came saying the sick boy was going to die because they feared it was caused by witchcraft. The father wanted to take him away. Jeanne asked for and received permission to move the boy into our medical clinic house. All the other people stayed away, fearing the disease was contagious. After taking the worm medicine, the sick boy sat on our little potty and passed a potty full of round worms. They had caused infection that was taken care of by the penicillin. The fever went down and he was well in just a few days.

Several days later, I worked with Kunyach reading the first three chapters of the Gospel of Mark in Spanish, trying to translate it into Aguaruna. We felt that we had accomplished a great deal.

On Sunday we had about fifty people at our house. We sang, then Alias gave the lesson he had prepared. After supper that evening, Tuyas and his wife, Lidia, came to visit us. Tuyas had made a crude, two-stringed violin for his amusement. He entertained us by playing his violin and singing in Aguaruna language, remarking, "Isn't the music pretty?" To us, a two-note song wasn't really pretty, though we were happy with him that he enjoyed making the music.

All day Monday we were busy packing to go downriver and visit other bilingual schools. Many people came to tell us goodbye, to get last minute medicine, or to buy trade goods (fish hooks, fish lines, matches, etc.). The next day we were up at dawn to eat breakfast and pack the final items. Kunyach saw to it that everything was loaded into the dugout canoe, then at midmorning we left for Uut downriver with Kunyach paddling. In all, we had seven people in the canoe besides our own belongings. We arrived at Yama Yakat, the Nazarene station, but no pastor was there. He had gone back to their headquarters on the coast. We floated in the swift current on down the Marañon to Uut, where teacher Shajian had his school. Most of the schools had 50-60 students, quite a job for these beginning teachers. Since many of these teachers learned to read in Spanish, a language they didn't know, many of them could read the words, but did not comprehend what they read. David Kunyach had been young enough that he read fairly fluently.

At Uut, Shajian and his wife welcomed us. His wife did not wear the sarong-style Aguaruna dress which left one shoulder bare. Having been to the coast among the Nazarenes with her husband, she wore western-style dress with short sleeves. She also did not cut bangs and short hair on the sides above the ears, which was the Aguaruna style for women's hair. The Nazarenes followed the biblical injunction that women's hair should all be long. One problem with women's long hair was that the long hair would get into the women's and babies' eyes and cause infection. Even for women with bangs and short hair at the sides, we treated many people, young and old, with bad eye infections. Frequently, people came to us for haircuts since we had good scissors.

The next morning I made breakfast, then went to have devotions in a quiet area by the water hole, a bubbling spring. Afterwards, I went to the school to observe teacher Shajian and some classes. He seemed very discouraged. I returned after the school day to help Shajian with his lesson plans and attendance book. I attempted to give Shajian some new ideas for teaching to encourage him.

Jeanne and I went across the river to visit Takayit. The women served us delicious meat and starchy manioc. Since we had to eat with our hands, it was necessary to wash our hands afterward. One adult student from the school had a comical sloth hat on. He jokingly said that he was going to wear it to kill the whites if they tried to take Aguaruna land. This had been the practice of the elderly Aguaruna men.

With so many students, it was hard for Shajian to give individual attention. I worked with him to divide the classes properly and suggested that he command attention and respect. We also rearranged seating to separate different grade levels and counted books to see how many more would be needed.

A young woman was brought to us doubled over with pain. She was lying on the ground in front of our doorway, vomiting and crying. She and her mother both said that she would die. Her family moved her to a little lean-to hut by the river, where she died the next day. Possibly she had taken *barbasco* poison and didn't tell us. In another case, a man in nearby Shushuinum fell in the river while fishing and drowned. Many people were dying for various reasons.

It had rained torrentially for four days there in Uut. Our radio had been off the air all week. It was under a piece of plastic out in the rain, and, when it quit raining, we weren't being heard. We could hear the base loud and clear, but they could not hear us. Our main radio was in Nazaret, but on our trip we had taken a more portable radio on which you sat and turned the handles on the small generator. Even though we had put up an antenna, it didn't work. Friday morning we decided that we had to go up to Nazaret to get on the air. We set out for upriver at midmorning with four joking teenagers, the barest of necessities, and a beautiful day. The boys joked around, but with their expertise at canoeing, we made the trip to Nazaret safely, arriving at eleven o'clock the next day. Jeanne made connection with the base on the main radio there, and we learned that a plane was at Yurimaguas on the way to check on us since they had not heard from us by radio all week. We sent the plane back to the base, telling them that we were fine.

Once again we traveled downriver by canoe, returning to Uut and taking the larger radio with us. There I saw that Shajian's school was operating much better than before. The boys began clearing the school grounds to make a volley ball court. Kunyach and his large party of canoes went by on the way back to Nazaret from getting salt downriver. We began packing to leave for Numpatkaim. I baked some bread to eat on our trip. After one last check at the bilingual school, we had lunch. The weather was good, so we packed and left in a canoe, accompanied by the raft we had started out with, piled high with supplies for the schools. The boys did a good job of piloting the canoe and raft. We arrived after a one or two hour trip to Numpatkaim. There we were provided with a nice, native-style house and even an outhouse. We asked boys to work for us, making fires and carrying water from the river. The friendly people brought delicious food, including an abundance of pineapples and bananas.

We heard that Mikayo, a young Aguaruna man at Kagkas, found his wife with another man, so, according to custom, Mikayo used his machete to make a long diagonal cut in the back at the base of their skulls. The purpose of this cut was not to kill the offenders but to leave a lifelong scar to mark them as adulterers. In desperation, the wife took *barbasco* poison and died, leaving the heartbroken husband to look for another wife.

Teacher Felipe went hunting on Sunday to find meat for his family. After he returned with his game, he had a meeting in which he read the Bible lesson from a Spanish Bible. He was an older man who had learned to read in Spanish, a language that he didn't speak fluently. That week we began checking the schools, Jeanne in teacher Mayan's school and I in Felipe's school most of the day. We helped them count books and take inventories. One school building was in such need of repair that Jeanne asked the older boys and men students to completely rebuild it.

A storm blew in with strong wind and rain. The boys' dorm roof was not finished yet, and palm leaves blew off. The boys pulled off their clothes and went out in the rain to repair it. The schoolboys had varied and interesting personalities. They came over to visit with us in the evening. I showed them pictures of my parents and siblings. Schoolboy Jaime brought his flute quite often, and we tried to write down words and music to Aguaruna songs.

One afternoon Jeanne and I went for a hike through the forest to visit the home of friend Moses' father. We were treated with gracious hospitality. His wife served us banana drink, of which I drank only a few swallows, but Jeanne drank a whole calabash bowl full. We visited a while, and they gave us papaya and bananas to take home. We took a swim to bathe here where anacondas were not found and then returned home. In the middle of the night, Jeanne woke up with upset stomach, diarrhea, and vomiting. The banana drink surely had some kind of bacteria in it. We cleaned her up and she was able to sleep the rest of the night. The next day Jeanne took sulfa drugs and stayed in bed most of the day. I made radio contact with Yarinacocha base, did house chores, and visited the schools. Jeanne was feeling better by the end of the day.

The moon was full at that time, giving us bright, moonlit nights. We went out in the schoolyard and played games with the children in the moonlight: flying Dutchman, dodge ball, and a few relays. Another night we went out in the moonlight to watch the boys practice for a school program. Puppet shows were popular at schools that year, too.

Testing was a new concept at the schools. Teacher Felipe needed a lot of help since he hadn't given tests before. The students wanted to look on each other's papers. Since they did not really understand the concept, I eventually sent two boys out of the class for cheating. The students worked math functions well, but wrote poorly, lacking writing books. The next day, after the tests were corrected, we went over the test papers in class.

On October eleventh, Jeanne and I spent the morning packing for the trip downriver past Chipi to Chicais. The Aguarunas loaded the two canoes and we set out on our trip. It began to pour down rain at Chipi. We waited a little while at Chipi, but soon decided we had better go on in the rain. I was covered with my raincoat and kept dry, but it was impossible to see the scenery in the heavy rain. We arrived at Chicais just at dusk. We hurried to unpack and settle for the night in the house of teacher Carlos.

The next day we set up the radio and learned that a plane was on its way with pilot Leo Lance to bring our SIL Canadian friend Annie Shaw for a visit. We prepared the house and baked some banana bread over the red-hot coals of the three-log fire. The plane arrived early enough in the afternoon to give us some time to visit various Aguaruna homes with Leo and Annie. At one home, we observed a handicapped Aguaruna man weaving the usual men's skirt with vertical stripes (the women's sarongs have horizontal stripes). We went to another home where an Aguaruna woman was making large, clay pots for cooking over the three-log fires. We also observed spinning cotton into thread. At another home, we were served delicious meat with starchy manioc to accompany it. We came across a sugar cane press that was similar to a North American old-fashioned hand water pump. However, the apparatus squeezed the sweet juice which came out of the spout, falling into a container below. Our final entertainment for Leo and Annie was observing a fast-moving soccer game with all players barefooted. We then served our guests a chicken dinner with manioc, plantain, and banana bread. Our friends retired early, but Jeanne and I stayed up until two o'clock in the morning, reading and answering precious mail from home which had been brought on the airplane. As always, it was great to hear from family and friends in the United States.

Since the next day was Sunday, after breakfast we had a time of Bible reading and fellowship in English. Before Annie and Leo left, we took a canoe trip and hike to see where oil was seeping out of the ground. A little before noon, pilot Leo decided it was time to fly the 600 miles back to Yarinacocha base.

That evening, teacher Daniel Dantuchu, brother to Alias Dantuchu of Nazaret, preached a good sermon at the Aguaruna Bible study. We taught them the two new songs in Aguaruna which they liked very much.

Our week was occupied with my work helping the teachers Carlos and Segundo with their record-keeping, while Jeanne treated seven men for leishmaniasis with daily painful injections. Some of the ulcers on their legs and feet were huge and putrid. I began to feel achy and weak about that time for some reason. A *mestizo* named Plenqui came by to talk with Jeanne about an influenza that was spreading down the river. He also talked with the Indians about it and filled them with fear.

That week we ate well. A leg of venison was brought to us as well as a nice large piece of fish to bake and a turtle served with beans. We were properly nourished even though we both felt achy like we were coming down with flu or something. We finally began taking sulfa drugs. Later, we found out that it was Asian flu that was going around the world. A few of the Aguarunas were sick, but not seriously. It did not develop as a plague until the next year.

Copies of Millie's book of Bible stories that she had translated were delivered to the schools. It spoke to the hearts of the teachers

*The Aguaruna Tribe*

and students alike. Teacher Daniel preached on weeknights and told about what it means to follow Jesus. Teacher Segundo came to talk with us about the problem of people drinking manioc beer. His wife made it and refused to stop even though he threw out each pot she made. Attendance at Bible studies increased from sixty people to seventy-five and, eventually, to eighty-two people. There were not only children, who liked singing songs, but also a number of older, long-haired men and their wives present. Daniel continued to preach well. First, just eight students decided they wanted to follow Jesus. Teacher Carlos came to us and said his heart was not right with God. We knelt and prayed with him as he confessed his sin. The next night seventeen students prayed and accepted the Lord Jesus Christ into their lives. Another night eight more students accepted the Lord. Their prayers were very scriptural and they seemed to really mean it. They coined the term 'Sell yourself out to God' for accepting Jesus Christ as Savior and Lord of one's life. We saw a total of forty people accept Christ as Savior. We hoped to see changed lives.

A motorboat came with a Peruvian lab technician and his crew to check the Indians' blood. We talked with him, then invited him to dinner, and he accepted. During dinner, he made a remark that we were sacrificing greatly to live among the Aguarunas. The next morning we made breakfast for him, then Jeanne went to work taking Aguaruna blood specimens for analysis. I helped by writing down names and organizing students. After the blood specimens were taken, the lab technician and his helpers left.

Some soldiers came from Cenepa downriver to lead the students in exercises. The soldiers were impressed by the performance of the students. Rainy season had arrived. Word came that Titus' canoe turned over in a huge whirlpool and all five people were in the water: two women, two babies, and Titus. They were all sucked to the bottom of the whirlpool while holding on to a long, tough vine tied to the bow of the canoe, then popped up to the surface, and were all saved. One mother forgot about the baby inside her dress, but the baby stayed inside and survived. The Marañon River was dangerously high since rainy season had begun.

We had a meeting of parents and teachers to talk over problems in the school, such as the need for discipline. It was interesting to see all the parents sitting on school benches with their colorful feathered crowns, bandoliers, and earrings. They spoke vigorously about problems and needs.

On the morning of November eleventh, we heard on the radio from Yarinacocha that a plane would be coming for us on November thirteenth. On that third day, Leo Lance reached Chicais by 11:45 in the morning. We had had two days to pack, so after dinner we had everything in the plane by 2:20 p.m. and left Chicais. The trip upriver by plane to Nazaret was thrilling because we could see a bird's eye view of all the schools we had visited along the river. We arrived at Nazaret at 2:45. Since the rivers were high, we landed on the Muchigkis River with port near our home. Jeanne talked with Kunyach and his son, teacher David. Jeanne packed away some of her equipment, then we took off in the plane, flying over the Marañon River downriver, passing over all the schools again, then landing at Napuruk downriver from Chicais. We were happily greeted by the Aguarunas, settled in, then had supper. That evening, about forty Indians gathered for a meeting. We taught this group the Aguaruna version of the song 'I Have Decided to Follow Jesus' and they also liked it very much. Teacher Moises led a discussion about spiritual matters.

Most of the next day Jeanne and I checked school records and observed teaching methods. It rained terribly hard all morning, but pilot Leo rounded up a chicken, killed it, and cooked it for lunch. After I did a little more work at the school, the sun came out and we hurried to pack and take off as soon as possible while the weather was nice. Leaving Napuruk, we flew east out of the foothills, then south over the vast green rain forest and along rivers, arriving at the town of Yurimaguas at 5:55 p.m., just five minutes under the six p.m. government deadline for flying in the rain forest. Being this close to the equator, the sun would go down right at six p.m. and there were no lighted landing strips. We stayed in the lovely home of North American Mennonite missionaries working in Spanish there. It was great to sleep in a real bed for the first time in a long time.

*The Aguaruna Tribe*

    After a delicious breakfast the next morning and with the plane refueled, we took off a little after nine o'clock on a cloudy day headed for Yarinacocha. We landed there on November 15 and had a great reunion with old friends. Jeanne and I spent two and one-half hours reporting to Dr. Efraim Morote Best, director of all the bilingual schools, about the progress of the Aguaruna schools and our experiences with the teachers.

# CHAPTER 13: THIRD TRIP TO THE AGUARUNA TRIBE

Exciting news was in the wind. On April 23, 1958, Jeanne Grover and I received word that in three days we would fly to Aguaruna country accompanied by *Life Magazine* photographer Cornell Capa. He was assigned to do the photography to illustrate an article about our work with the Aguaruna. We immediately began to rush to complete a month's work in three days preparing for the trip. I was working in publications typing Jeanne's Aguaruna health book, besides packing for the trip. Three days later the morning dawned foggy and misty. Our time for takeoff was set for nine o'clock. I transferred my packed belongings down to the plane at the river. After goodbyes, we were finally off the water of Lake Yarinacocha in the Norseman with pilot Ted Long and co-pilot Jim Baptista at 10:20 a.m. The first hour we encountered heavy rain and ominous clouds, a threat of a tropical storm. After flying low over the Ucayali River, we landed at Oriente, a small Peruvian village. The weather soon improved, so the pilot refueled, and we flew overland to Angamos on the Marañon River.

Jeanne and I wrote notes for our family letters that would be mailed after the plane's return trip to Yarinacocha. The plane was so noisy that we couldn't converse, but Cornell Capa observed everything closely, occasionally commenting on the extremely hot and humid weather. In the afternoon, we left Angamos for Chikais in beautiful weather with lots of silver-lined clouds to the west where we were headed. We passed the first chain of mountains, flying over the *Pongo de Manseriche* whirlpools, then following the twisting Marañon River up in mountainous Aguaruna country to land on the river at Chicais. The pilot had a hard time taxiing over into the mouth of Chicais stream because the major river's current was so strong. A grand number of Aguaruna people lined the riverside to greet us. The Aguaruna men had built a large thatch-roofed Aguaruna-style house for us. There was a kitchen and bedroom for us, and a pilot's room with door opening only to the outside. Jeanne and I

*The Aguaruna Tribe*

unpacked and blew up our air mattresses, then set up the kitchen for cooking. The photographer began taking pictures soon after arrival, highlighting our work and the activities of the Aguarunas in a trip around the area. The next day the pilots, along with Cornell Capa, decided to leave at four o'clock in the afternoon. They had some tense moments in their take-off from the swift, swollen Marañon River, but they finally were in the air and on their way out of the foothills to spend the night at Angamos.

The day after the plane left, we had Aguaruna men working for us. They built cane-pole and palm-bark medical shelves, a radio shelf, pantry shelves, and dressing room benches in our thatched roof house. The dressing room was a seven-foot square room, consisting of pink cloth hung so that we would have privacy to dress and undress. The cane pole walls were usually lined with young and old people outside peeking in to try to see what we white women were doing. The benches were just four forked poles planted in the ground with pieces of palm bark to sit on. We also put up plastic for a ceiling over the kitchen table to keep dirt or vampire bat droppings from falling into our food.

The Aguarunas showed great interest in spiritual matters. Tito asked Jeanne if she had brought God's Word, but Millie was still on furlough, so no further translation had been accomplished. Jeanne did sell fifty hymnbooks which were joyfully purchased.

We hiked over to Grandma Majik's garden to get some okra. She had quite a sense of humor. Some of the older women felt our breasts through our clothes to make sure we were women, since we were so well covered with clothing. On the way home, we picked beautiful wild flowers and wild fruit.

The next day was radio day, our day to receive base and world news. It helped us to feel less isolated. Afterward I sewed some dishtowels by hand since the termites ate up our old ones.

Chicais was a village with four school buildings and four teachers: Daniel Dantuchu, Danny Chamikit, as well as Segundo and Carlos, for whom we did not know their last names (fathers' names). May first was a school holiday, so all the teachers went hunting to feed their families. We had chicken dinner since Pyuch didn't want to keep feeding an old chicken that wouldn't lay eggs.

We set regular store and medical hours. We had a small supply of trade goods that we either exchanged for food or sold to the people, though it was not really a store. It was hard to keep regular hours since people kept coming to visit and to share with us their papaya, palm heart, avocados, manioc, peanuts, and meat from wild animals. In the evening Daniel Dantuchu came with a male student to discuss the problem of those young men who take two or three girls as wives and then abandon one or two of them. Having multiple wives was a practice in their culture. Peruvian law dictates that a man must have only one wife, and also the New Testament teaches the same, but wives can't be abandoned without caregivers. Daniel was good at counseling with students about their problems.

Saturday was 'odds and ends' day. Several students worked for us from nine o'clock in the morning until noon. They cut brush around our house, made a fence, and built a typing table in the main visiting room. As with other furniture, the typing table legs were planted in the dirt floor. Jeanne had thirty-five patients that day. We mixed up some rat poison and sent it out to various houses since rats are carriers of the disease leishmaniasis. The whole week had been a time of settling and adjusting to the area.

Together Jeanne and I began the study in English of St. Paul's letter to the Ephesians. "Live lives worthy of your high calling. Accept life with humility and patience, making allowances for each other because you love each other. Make it your aim to be at one in the Spirit, and you will inevitably be at peace with one another." (Ephesians 4:1-2 in Phillips' translation) There were 115 Aguarunas at the evening service. Daniel Dantuchu read the Scriptures, then gave a few applications and exhortations which were well received.

We had a meeting with the teachers to discuss problems in the schools and communities on Monday. David Kunyach from Nazaret, Segundo and Danny Chamikit all said they had not turned their lives over to the Lord. Daniel Dantuchu shows real spiritual insight and a concern for the spiritual status of each person. After the teachers' meeting, the mayors, who had been elected and appointed for each community, crowded into a school building. They were all older men who had the typical Aguaruna long hair and wore skirts. They had all built small jailhouses in their communities. This town meeting

*The Aguaruna Tribe*

was about planting a rubber tree grove. They were dressed in their feathered finery and, as is custom, all shouted their comments at once, a noisy, but important, meeting. In the evening, the teachers came to proofread the health book Jeanne had written.

The next day I went to school to see about decreasing the number of students. Since classrooms were crowded, I went to the school to see if there was a way to decrease the number of students per class. I found there were many children seven or eight years old that could wait until the next year. There were young men in the classes who had no previous opportunity to study. Some wanted to take advantage of the opportunity to go to school in spite of having to care for their families.

On May 12 I had my twenty-seventh birthday. I felt bad, so I ate breakfast, washed the dishes, and went back to bed. By noon I felt better, and I prepared dinner, then typed the Spanish for specific school Bible Scriptures that were required in primary school books by the Peruvian Ministry of Education. Millie would have to translate these into Aguaruna after she would come back from her graduate studies.

Daniel Dantuchu gave the students a lesson on creation on Sunday morning. The afternoon meeting for adults proved to be quite interesting. There were twelve women, four older men, and the four teachers present. The lesson was again on creation with some interesting discussion. Two *masato* beer-drinking parties attracted most of the people accounting for the low attendance at the Bible study.

One Saturday we went with the school children on an excursion to see a man weaving, since it was the men who did the weaving in this tribe. One of his legs had been amputated, leaving him handicapped, but able to do the sit-down job of weaving. He lived alone up on a ridge about a twenty-minute hike away from the Chicais settlement. Returning from the visit, Jeanne and I went for a bath in the Chicais creek on that beautiful, sunny, quiet day. Feeling refreshed after bathing, we worked on her health book corrections.

Twelve boys and a man named Wamputsan gathered to pray one Wednesday night. The boys all prayed from their hearts. Since Jeanne was out of penicillin, we prayed that the plane would come bringing a new supply. Also, they prayed that Dr. Morote Best, director of the bilingual schools, would do a good job of overseeing the schools and about other community problems.

At the end of the week, most of the teachers were gone: Daniel and David to Urakusa, Segundo to the army post at Alianza downriver, and Danny Chamikit to hunt food in the forest for his family. A good student named Zacarias came to our house at two o'clock in the afternoon to practice reading the Bible lesson for Sunday. He did a good job, reading with understanding and excellent expression.

The Chicais mayor came over in the evening with another leishmaniasis patient for Jeanne to give injections. With him also were the mayor's young daughter and a student named Pepe, who was brought for a trial. Pepe was accused of disturbing the girl in the night, pulling up her dress with intentions of attacking her sexually. Pepe denied it, saying that he had been an evangelical Christian under Mr. Douglass at the Nazarene mission at Yama Yakat, but backslid and went back to drinking. Later, Pepe was found guilty and whipped in front of the school students. He recognized and admitted his sin before the group.

One day we were left at Chicais with the children and elderly women while the other men and women all went out for the day. Jeanne and I dressed in Aguaruna sarongs which had been dyed a light brown color with dyes from the forest. We also had our faces painted and went visiting at four houses. The women were good hostesses, giving us palm heart at one house, fish at another, and wild potatoes at another. When all the other adults returned, they were surprised and pleased to see our attire.

At midnight, teacher Danny Chamikit woke us, calling fellow teacher Segundo to say that he heard a spirit walking around. Segundo said he heard it also. They couldn't sleep most of the night, fearing the strange noises they heard which sounded like plastic being shaken. The next day, someone made a trip to the cooperative storehouse filled with hanging deer and wild hog hides hanging from the ceiling, as well as balls of rubber. Unbeknown to the people, a dog had been closed in the storehouse for the night, jumping up to reach the animal hides and causing the mysterious "spirit" noises. The storehouse, or warehouse, was a large, palm-

*The Aguaruna Tribe*

thatched roof building with walls on all sides, having only one door that could be closed. Inside were stored the hides and rubber which Daniel would take to Iquitos on the Amazon River at the end of the school year. Taking the items to Iquitos was an effort to avoid being cheated by traders on the rivers who paid the Indians low prices for their goods and charged them exorbitant prices for trade goods. We had helped Daniel set up bookkeeping to keep accounts of who had brought hides or rubber in order to pay them back properly after the merchandise was sold.

On a rainy Sunday, there were about fifty Aguarunas present to listen to the Bible story from the book Millie translated. Zacarias led the study and did quite well. Jeanne helped the students memorize John 3:16 in Aguaruna. After the meeting, I worked on trying to compose a gospel song. Suddenly, there was a quick earthquake that shook the house. We all ran outside, but there were no other shocks. The Indians did not seem to be afraid.

Dawuch and his wife came over to see us. His wife said she wanted to talk with us about the gospel because she was afraid to talk in front of all the other people. She wanted to "sell herself out to God" as they said it.

Thursday dawned a beautiful day in Chicais. After the weather cleared at Lake Capirona (Shapraland) about noon, pilot Bernie May flew from there to Chicais in the Aeronca. We served the pilots an all-native dinner consisting of chicken, manioc, pineapple, and avocado. After dinner, Jeanne and Bernie flew up to Nazaret to tell Kaikat to come downriver, gathering all the Indian teachers along the way as he would come, for a meeting. They returned at five o'clock in the afternoon.

Pilot Bernie and the co-pilot, with our helper Jorge, flew down to Urakusa and Napuruk the next day to have the land grant papers signed there. This was very important to give the Indians ownership of their own land so that when the road came through they would be able to defend their land from the white people. After lunch the teachers began arriving from upriver. They signed the land grant papers and provided information about their schools and communities to send to Yarinacocha base. By four o'clock all the information was complete, allowing pilot Bernie to take off since the weather was beautiful. He would deliver these papers to officials who would take them to Lima.

We watched a soccer game between Chicais students and the upriver teachers. Chicais won the game 5-2. In the evening all sixteen teachers (more than twice as many as there had been) and Kaikat came over to our house for a meeting to discuss problems in the schools and communities. The animated discussion at our house went on until eleven o'clock at night, then moved to the cooperative building and went on almost all night. The cultural changes and problems were multiplying with the new bilingual schools and preparations for the coming of the road with many white settlers. At breakfast time, all the teachers came to buy trade goods. Then Alias left in his motorized boat, the other teachers paddled away in their dugout canoes, and the rest of the morning was calm.

# *CHAPTER 14: DEATH, FEAR, AND EPIDEMIC*

The previous night, Jeanne had slipped out of the meeting to give medicine to a sick student named Laurenzio across the Chicais stream. By the next evening, we realized how ill Laurenzio was. He was dehydrated and lacked body salts due to extreme vomiting and diarrhea. He was having terrible muscle cramps and his eyes were sunken. Not knowing if he would live, we stayed with him until eleven o'clock that night. Two Chicais teachers stayed with him all night.

The next day was Sunday, and Jeanne stayed with Laurenzio. I went up to the Bible story meeting where fifty students were present. Cristobal did an excellent job of leading the meeting, giving a lesson on Noah and the ark, and using Millie's translation of Bible stories as a source book. We prayed for Laurenzio and made the application of being ready to meet God in death, as well as discussing the rainbow and how it doesn't have anything to do with the anaconda. They had worshipped the rainbow boa constrictor and its heavenly form, the rainbow. In the afternoon adult Bible study, David Kunyach from Nazaret told some of the stories he had learned in translating the book of Genesis with Jeanne.

During the day, Jeanne stayed with Laurenzio, giving him small drinks of saline solution to restore his body salts and hinder dehydration. On Monday he seemed to be somewhat improved, keeping fluids down and without muscle pain. We considered this an answer to prayer.

Later, Yuyua was brought to our house from Yama Yakat, the Nazarene Mission. He was terribly ill and weak from two weeks of malaria. Relatives who brought him downriver by canoe put him in the pilot's room of our house. Because his temperature was 103.4 degrees, Jeanne gave him aspirin and medicine for malaria. In late afternoon his brother washed him well since he had been without a bath for nine days (and he smelled like it). At the same time, a little boy named Intap was brought to us. He had a knot of roundworms in his stomach with infection and fever, prompting Jeanne to take care of him most of the day. She also gave twenty or more Repodral injections for leishmaniasis patients. A busy day!

It was as if a bombshell hit when we were told the next day that both Tyiats and Samekash were in critical condition. We hiked quickly a half-hour up the ridge. Tyiats was lying on a board, eyes glazed, mouth open, body twitching and muscles cramping. A little farther along the path Samekash was lying on a pallet, eyes sunken, stomach heaving, body twitching and trembling. They were both carried down to Laurenzio's house and placed on pallets to be cared for together. We gave them both Paregoric to stop vomiting and saline solution to restore their body salts. We massaged their muscles and finally in the afternoon they were both resting quite well. Tyiats vomited what looked like blood. He continued to stare with mouth open, to say his chest hurt, and that he was going to die. But he was quieted down, resting, and seemed improved.

Late in the afternoon Samekash began to vomit again and this continued all night. Students took turns sitting with them while we ate and slept. Jeanne kept giving twenty daily injections to leishmaniasis patients. Yuyua, in our house, seemed little improved of his malaria, which did not have the typical malaria schedule of rising and falling fever, but which rose erratically. We watched the two sick men Tyiats and Samekash across the Chicais stream until midnight, then went home, exhausted, to sleep.

After breakfast the next morning, someone ran up to our house breathlessly telling us that Tyiats was dead! We rushed across the creek and ran to the house where we beheld a grievous, horrible sight. The body of Tyiats was stretched out on the ground behind the house with that same wide-eyed stare and open mouth, accented by the pall of death. Misankit was wailing loudly and uncontrollably by his side. We were stunned and stood there with heads bowed and hearts bleeding, while people around us wept, wailed, and shouted. Misankit explained that Tyiats said he had to defecate so she helped him outside and he fell down and died. She was wild with grief, trying to choke herself and wildly throwing herself about. Tyiats' body was carried to the family house nearby, and many Aguaruna went to view the body and wail, a plaintiff melody that echoed across the hills. We were told that Tyiats had eaten a bowl of spoiled food the day before he began vomiting.

With all the noise and wailing, Samekash began to vomit again. He looked so pathetic, lying in his own vomit on his little pallet on the ground, covered by dirty clothes. The paregoric didn't faze his unmerciful heaving. Jeanne gave him a penicillin injection, but he vomited pieces of fish along with blood, so we felt that he also, indeed, had food poisoning, as we had been told. The people felt disgusted toward us since the small amount of medicine and saline solution that Jeanne gave him did no good. Three of the men carried his weak, wretched body to a canoe and paddled him down to the army fort at Alianza. The next morning, news came that the canoe was coming back upriver and that the people in it were wailing. We knew that Samekash had died, and felt as if arrows were shot into our hearts! The hills echoed and reechoed with wailing all around us. Our feelings were inexpressable. We walked as if in a stupor. Late that morning Daniel returned from upriver. All the people gathered around him and told the news of the deaths, then the three of us went to our house and had a long talk about what had happened. I couldn't keep from crying, though teacher Daniel was quite a comfort.

The death of the two men brought fear to the rest of the people. They imagined that they were coming down with the illness the two men had. They came in droves asking for medicine. Forty patients came that day, and used almost all our medicine. Again the next day, medical patients came all morning. We satisfied them psychologically by giving them aspirin and even vitamins, the only kinds of pills we had left.

The Sunday morning service was held at the schoolboys' dormitory with about sixty students present. Also present was sorrowing teacher Danny Chamikit, who was related to the men who died, and our helper, Jorge, who regularly brought our water supply from the river and made fires for boiling water. Daniel presented the story of why Jesus came to suffer and die for the sins of the world. He spoke about suffering and death, striking close to home in those days when the feel of death was still in the air. We still heard wailing for the deceased.

The adult service was a repeat of the creation lesson, using a world globe to illustrate the round earth and where the Aguaruna are located. The people from Nazaret who were relatives of the deceased were present. Daniel Dantuchu had an evening meeting with fifty-two people attending. He spoke about heaven, where there is no sorrow, no sickness, and streets of gold.

Yujua continued to puzzle us. He had no pain, but had fever all the time, going up to 101, 102, and 103 degrees every day, while almost never down to normal. He had been given about every kind of treatment possible. Jeanne had a radio talk with Dr. Eichenberger, mostly about Yujua. Doc was also puzzled because the regular up-and-down fevers of malaria were not present. Along with treating Yujua, Jeanne was also injecting thirty Aguaruna leishmaniasis patients daily. The pain of the shots made even grown men cry.

I completed teacher Danny Chamikit's attendance sheet since he would not want to write the names of his deceased relatives. It is Aguaruna custom not to speak or write a deceased relative's name for about a year. I visited the other schools in Chicais to count and sort extra books for needy schools in other villages.

The Father Superior of the priests and nuns downriver at the *mestizo* town of Nieva came by to visit briefly. He spoke English and was quite inquisitive and friendly. At the same time, the long-haired elderly Aguaruna mayors of all the villages up and down the river arrived for a meeting. They met on a Saturday night from seven to eleven o'clock, talking, shouting, and gesticulating as they discussed forms of punishment for broken Aguaruna customs and other problems as well as simply giving reports from their areas.

Following the two deaths, there were a number of diarrhea and vomiting cases that convinced us that an influenza epidemic was taking place. One Aguaruna man who went hunting a couple of days away became ill and couldn't walk to return. Daniel and some school students went after him and brought him back. Before we ran out, we gave him some diarrhea medicine and he began improving, although he was weak and dehydrated. There were also three other people from his house sick with diarrhea. Early the next morning ten people were at our door with complaints of sore abdomen, diarrhea, and nausea. We were out of paregoric, sulfa, carbisone, and enteroyioform. Nurse Jeanne vomited that night and didn't feel good. The airplane was to leave for Shapra country that day, so I told the base radio operator I considered it urgent that the doctor come to us and bring medicine. We were greatly relieved when we received a response that the doctor and medicines were on their way.

At eleven o'clock the next morning, the plane came. Doc hurriedly examined all the sick people and brought ample supplies of medicine. Cornell Capa, *Life Magazine* photographer, came also and stood in the sidelines taking pictures. They were all gone by 12:45 p.m. and it was like a dream that they had been there. I helped Jeanne with fifty-one patients in all, thirty of them diarrhea patients. The next day we had sixty patients as the intestinal flu epidemic continued. Many people were so fearful of becoming ill that they just imagined that they were ill. Because of the flu epidemic, I directed the work crews to wash down all the school tables and benches with disinfectant. Jeanne continued treating the twenty leishmaniasis patients even through the flu epidemic. These patients required as many as forty or fifty injections each to be cured of the dreadful disease.

We were having heavy rain at that time, and the river was high. The cold and rainy period, in what would normally be dry season, came up from the South Pole annually approximately June $24^{th}$ through the $26^{th}$. It was called *San Juan*, Saint John, because he was the saint celebrated at that period of time.

After he returned to the base, Dr. Eichenburger radioed back to us that our patient Yujua had vivex malaria which had loaded his spleen and kept releasing more malaria into his blood stream in an irregular fashion. We gave him regular heavy doses of malaria medicine and he gradually improved. About two weeks later he was cured, fever-free, and went home. We were very happy for him.

Teacher Moises from downriver at Napuruk spent about two hours telling us about the problems of Jum who lived there. Jum had brought his rubber and hides to the cooperative at Chikais which would bypass the mestizo trader with whom he usually did business. When the Spanish-speaking trader asked Jum where his rubber and hides were, not knowing Spanish Jum only said, "*Señoritas cooperativo.*" Enraged because Jum wouldn't do business with him, the trader gravely punished him by cutting his hair off, beating him, and burning different parts of his body with coals from the fire, among other bad treatment. We heard of his maltreatment, but it was a few weeks before he was healed enough to come upriver to Chikais to see us and Daniel to tell of his horrible experiences.

One day some Aguarunas from northeast in Huambisa territory brought to us a woman and a small girl. They said that there was a Japanese man who sexually molested Aguaruna women and small girls. The men wanted us to see about punishing the Japanese man. He had paid off the law in the *mestizo* town of Nieva and there were no other Peruvian lawmen to deal with him. We were sorry to have to tell our visitors there was nothing we could do for them.

After all the weeks of illness and sadness, we had some pleasant times. I continued to type on Jeanne's Scripture translations she had accomplished while working with David. Late in the afternoon we went for a bath, then took a short canoe trip up the Chicais stream. I steered while Jeanne paddled and poled most of the way. There were two little boys and two giggly girls with us to make our outing interesting.

Moises came up from Napuruk, bringing with him a bilingual young man who was born Aguaruna but raised as a *mestizo*. We talked with him Saturday evening and again Sunday morning finding out his background as a bilingual person. He had spent some time in the Peruvian navy, but wanted to be a bilingual teacher. Eventually, he did accomplish his goal.

We received word by radio that a group of Christian businessmen from Oklahoma would be coming out to visit us with their leader, Amos Baker. The schoolboys worked hard making beds for the visitors, clearing the soccer field, and making paths clear and wide. I typed all morning and worked with Daniel and David on the cooperative's records in the afternoon. Continuing cases of diarrhea were already depleting Jeanne's stock of medicine again. We prepared further for the coming of the seven Christian businessmen, WBT/SIL Peru Branch Director Harold Goodall, and pilot Don Smith. They arrived on Thursday, July 3 with all their cameras and gear. We gave them a tour of the area: the drinking water spring; the cooperative building with exhibits of basket weaving, clay pot making, broom making, belt weaving, and ornamental outfit making. Following this, the Aguarunas gave a dancing exhibition.

After dinner, the Aguarunas had an evening meeting for our visitors. A few of the school students gave short talks about becoming Christians that were translated into English. Then a few of the businessmen spoke in English about their experiences in their Christian lives, with Jeanne translating into Aguaruna. Forty Aguarunas responded to the invitation to give their lives to Jesus Christ. The North American businessmen rejoiced. After the meeting, the businessmen had cake and coffee at our house, during which Jeanne and I told them some of our tribal experiences.

On Friday, July 4 (not a holiday in Peru), eleven of us had a hearty breakfast. The school children presented a short program. They sang, raised the Peruvian flag, and recited some Scriptures in Aguaruna for the North American men, who took pictures. Finally, the men filed through a palm-lined path down to the river, loaded into a canoe, and left for the plane. Before the pilots canoed to their plane, we showed them the boys' dorm houses and soccer field. Jeanne and I took the next three days to rest and recover from the days of preparations and entertaining.

The following Sunday morning and evening meetings were well attended by ninety Aguarunas each time. Thankfully, we were back to what one might call a normal routine. I spent most of the day preparing records of Jeanne's patients with leishmaniasis. Afterward, Daniel and I spent time translating Proverbs chapter six. The school students were memorizing poetry in Spanish and practicing for the Peruvian Independence Day program to be held on July 28.

Three students, Augustin, Shimpu, and Jorge, were punished for adultery, which was not allowed in Aguaruna culture. The Chicais mayor and lieutenant mayor each whipped them. Jorge was unrepentant and arrogant. He was discovered having sex with his half sister, even though they were both married to other people. Shimpu, brother of teacher Segundo, was living with Lucila, a widow aunt by marriage. The mayor gave them a loud lecture and made them get married. Augustin had tried to have an affair with one of Yujua's two sisters, but awakened the wrong sister in the night. After the boys had been dealt with, Daniel read and preached from Proverbs, chapter six (warnings against adultery) and First Peter chapter five, verse eight (be self-controlled and alert).

I continued charting leishmaniasis patients since Jeanne was so far behind on medical records. Afterward, I again worked on translation, this time in First John, chapter one, verses five through ten about good characteristics of the Christian life: faith, virtue, knowledge, temperance, patience, godliness, brotherly kindness, and love.

Just as David came to work with Jeanne on translation one morning, student Walter discovered that David's wife, Victoria, was missing. After some investigation, it was disclosed that Wampukai had taken her away. Some young men were sent to get her, but they returned empty-handed in early afternoon. Wampukai had pointed his gun at them, and they were not able to do anything. Then David and eight students went upriver and retrieved his wife.

Santus brought to us his baby boy who was very sick with vomiting. The mother was afraid and crying, but Jeanne treated the baby and he improved greatly. We were called to see a woman named Ensamai who was lying down bleeding profusely. We decided she must have a tumor. She was a believer in Jesus. We sedated her and she was quiet, but the hemorrhaging began again and continued the rest of the night. The Aguarunas had a type of red medicine from the forest that they used on her and it worked. The hemorrhaging stopped though she was still in pain. She did eventually recover, for which we were thankful.

I realized that life in the tribe had been one long series of crises and emergencies for the last three months. Every time we had one victory for the Lord, Satan would bring another critical situation to hinder the translation work and spiritual counseling of the many new believers.

Two of the men were crying because their wives had been taken away by their in-laws. We had a big palaver going on in our house with both sides shouting out loudly in typical Aguaruna fashion. Agreement was finally reached.

Cases of diarrhea and vomiting from the flu virus kept popping up, but the great fear of it had passed. I continued to record the patient information, listed all the debts and typed up slips of paper to

*The Aguaruna Tribe*

hand out informing Aguarunas of their medical debts. The majority paid with eggs, chickens, manioc, plantain, bananas, or pineapples which we enjoyed eating.

On July 18 it rained hard most of the morning, but we packed our belongings and left Chikais at two o'clock in the afternoon by canoe with some of our belongings on a balsa raft, bound for a stay at Urakusa. We stopped at the army post Alianza for half an hour's visit. By then it was a beautiful, sunny day. Once again on the clear, swift river, we came to Pongo Nuevo, the huge whirlpool, but made it safely past. We arrived at Urakusa by sundown and received a warm welcome.

At 6:30 in the morning, Daniel and the Chikais students left for home upriver against the current. We set up our kitchen and enjoyed the quietness and restfulness as compared with the larger village, Chikais. The Indians killed a deer and gave us some deer meat that we thoroughly enjoyed. Our supplies were low, so we were thankful for every provision.

Sunday was a beautiful, sunny day. Most of the people were gone to other locations, so we had a real day of rest. The few men in the village killed two more deer so that we had more meat than we could eat. We shared it with the Indians. We enjoyed listening to HCJB Christian shortwave radio out of Quito, Ecuador.

During school recreation time the next morning, we had a very exciting deer chase. The deer, hiding in the brush of the riverbank, was scared out but ran up the port steps to the top, then back down. It went up the bank a second time, but no one shot it because there were dozens of school children chasing it. The deer finally ran into the river, where some men in a canoe paddled furiously, overtook it, and killed it.

After only four days at Urakusa, we packed, ate lunch, and were ready to load the balsa rafts. Just as we had all our supplies on the beach and were loading the two balsa rafts, the sky opened and rain began to pour. Although it continued pouring rain, we finished loading and left for Napuruk, two balsa rafts floating downriver. Kunyach and his men from distant Nazaret were accompanying us. We were protected by our ponchos, but the Aguarunas were soaked and cold. We arrived at Napuruk at sundown. The house assigned to us had a palm bark floor with separate bedrooms for each of us. How luxurious! Kunyach and his men began their long journey home upriver in rain and darkness. Later, we heard that on the way their canoe was overturned in a small whirlpool, losing a pair of shoes and some money. We were thankful to hear of their safe arrival in spite of their problems.

In Napuruk, we had excellent radio contact with the base during which we learned that the plane wouldn't come for two more days. Our supplies were scant, barely enough to last. We had only manioc and bananas for food. Also, some men brought us palm heart larvae, which we valued for protein, to toast in the fire.

The bilingual school teachers needed my help, occupying me while Jeanne ministered to the people's medical needs. At our meeting with adults and students, they were greatly interested in learning the songs from the new song books. The students sang Aguaruna hymns in the moonlight, with various groups singing together, giving the effect of rounds. After the singing, we had a meeting on our front porch with mostly school children attending. Jeanne read about the birth of Jesus from the recently translated Bible verses. August gave a very good talk telling the complete way to have a changed life.

The day that the plane was to arrive, we packed all our belongings. However, at noon we were informed that the plane would return to Yurimaguas for the night, making it necessary for us to unpack our bedding. Our food supply was gone: no milk, flour, oil or canned goods. We were eating manioc and bananas three times a day. I worked on school attendance and matriculation records. The next day we received word that the Grummond Duck plane would pick us up around noon. Since the plane's radio wasn't functioning, nothing could be heard from them between ten-thirty in the morning and two o'clock in the afternoon. When we finally heard from the pilots, they were circling over Lake Capirona in Shapra country in the midst of a terrible rain storm. Our supplies were all packed and ready to go. At four o'clock the pilot radioed that he was ten minutes away. We quickly dispatched everything across the river in canoes. As the plane arrived, six canoes were crossing the Marañon River. When the river was clear, the Duck plane landed and pulled up on a gravel beach at the far end of the island. Pilot Ralph Borthwick, radio operator Ray Isbell, and Mennonite Brethren missionary Bert Elliot from Yurimaguas deplaned and helped load the plane. We said a sad goodbye to the Aguarunas and the plane took off from the water at 5:00 p.m. We flew as the crow flies rather than following the river, arriving in Angamos at 5:40 p.m., just under the six o'clock deadline for flying over the rain forest. The men refueled the plane and worked on a *mestizo*'s generator to help him out. We ate a supper of boiled eggs and cold beans at eleven o'clock that night, then went to bed. I had two pillows for a mattress since little of our bedding was available.

On Sunday, July 27, 1958, we took off at 8:30 a.m. for Yurimaguas. The flight was a safe one, arriving in good time. We attended a meaningful communion service with the Brethren group, then a scrumptious roast beef dinner with all the trimmings prepared by the Elliot and Coenhoven families. After some interesting conversation, at 3:15 p.m. we took off for Yarinacocha, flying at 10,000 feet. The sadness of leaving behind our Aguaruna brethren was overcome by our delight in seeing our friends and co-workers at the base. Our exciting months among the Aguaruna would be shared with many others. We had many to thank for their prayers.

# *PART IV: CASHIBO-CACATAIBO*

MAP PLATE 3

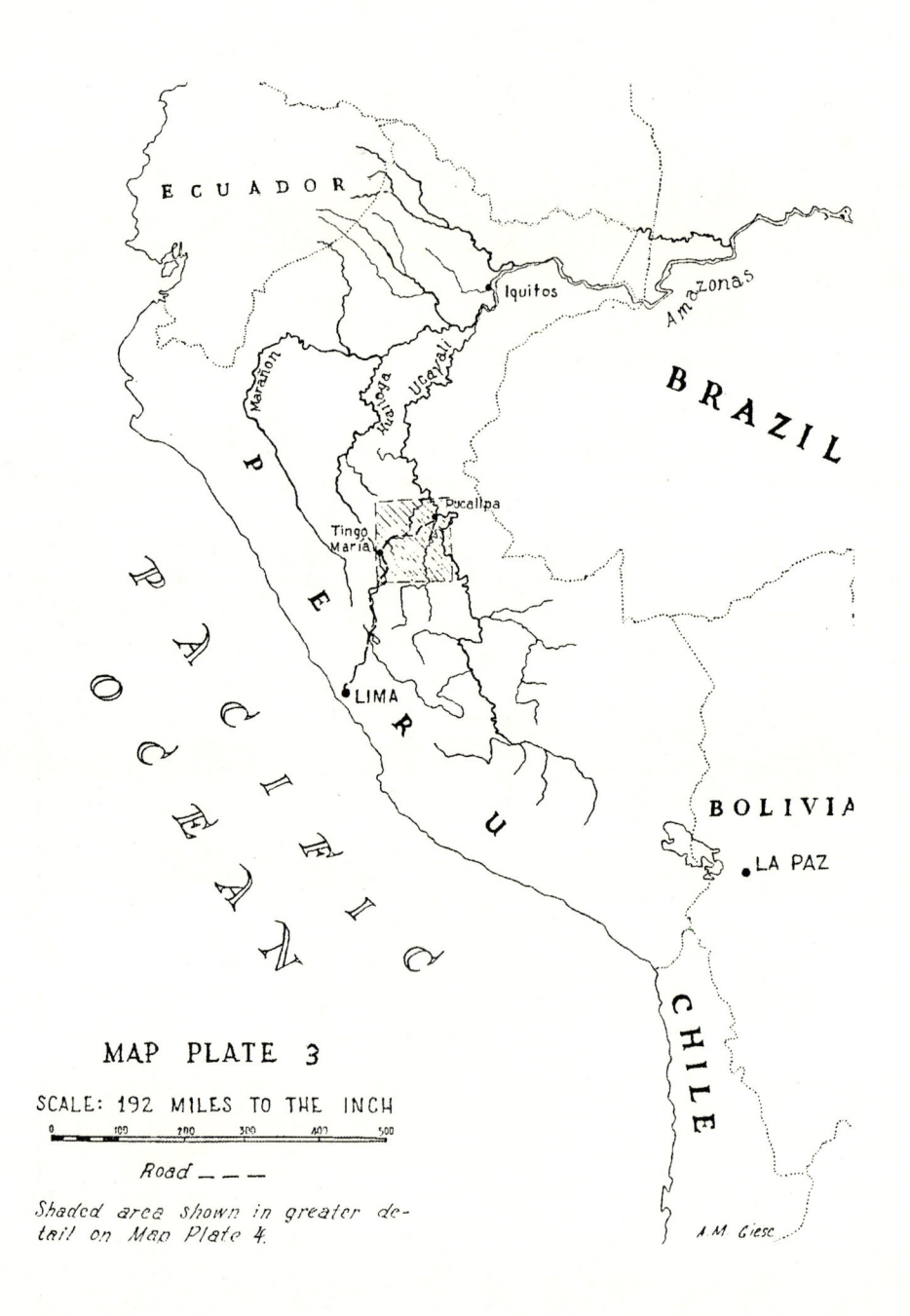

SCALE: 192 MILES TO THE INCH

Road _ _ _

Shaded area shown in greater detail on Map Plate 4.

**MAP PLATE 4**

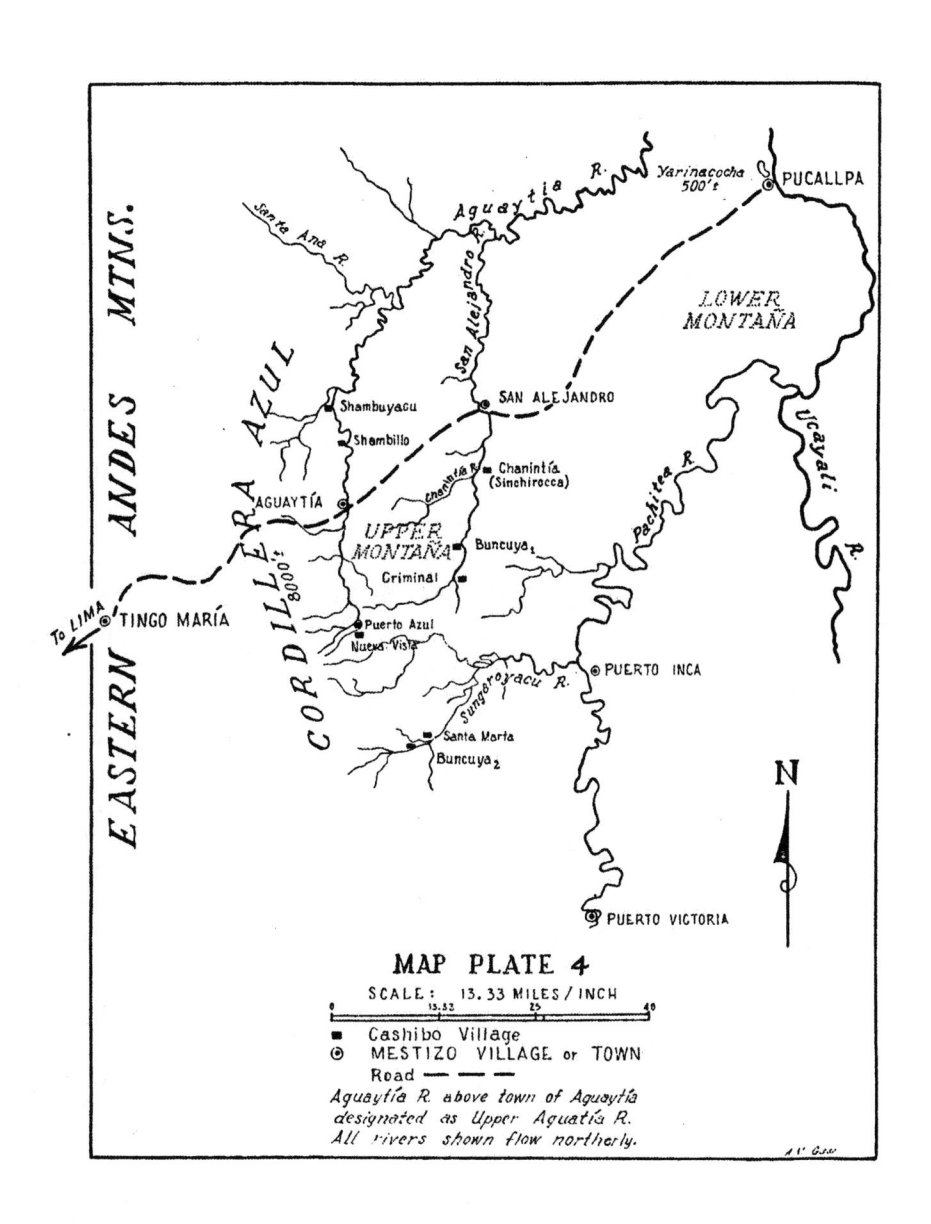

SCALE: 13.33 MILES / INCH

■ Cashibo Village
⊙ MESTIZO VILLAGE or TOWN
Road ———

*Aguaytía R. above town of Aguaytía designated as Upper Aguatía R. All rivers shown flow northerly.*

# *CHAPTER 15: ASSIGNED TO THE CASHIBO-CACATAIBO TRIBE*

In December of 1957, I went to talk with the Base director, Harold Goodall. I hesitated to enter work with the Cashibo-Cacataibo tribe, but Harold urged me to go ahead. I decided to trust the Lord to be with me and my partner, Irma Schaal. The Lord immediately gave me joy and peace, and a feeling of being in the center of His will.

Olive Shell from Canada had become a member of WBT/SIL on January 1, 1944. She and member Gloria Gray from Arkansas entered the Cashibo tribe on the Aguaytia River in the mid-1940's. They had studied the language well, giving it an alphabet and preparing several Cashibo primers for the bilingual schools in downriver Shambuyacu, upriver Pintayo, and at the San Alejandro River location where the people were named "Cacataibo."

Olive published a marvelous linguistic article laying out the morphemes (small words or parts of words with meaning) of Cashibo-Cacataibo in charts showing the order of these meaningful units. Gloria made a first draft translation of the Gospel of Mark. Both saw some of the tribespeople come to know Jesus as their Savior from sin. However, in 1953 Gloria married James Wroughton, who worked with SIL International as government contact man. Gloria bid the Cashibo-Cacataibo goodbye and set up her new home in Lima, the capital city of Peru. That left Olive Shell without a partner. In 1955 Olive earned an MA degree from The University of Michigan.

On December 25, 1957, while living in the girls' dorm, I helped Olive with Christmas dinner for about eleven Cashibo-Cacataibo at her house. Olive told the Christmas story in their language, we had a simple meal, then just talked and visited. Later in the day, we had a single folks' party at the home of some base workers.

A week later I moved from the girls' dorm to Olive's house. The church in Houston had provided for me a wonderful three-quarter size kerosene refrigerator which was put to use in Olive's small, but comfortable, screened-in house with no glass windows. The house had a living room, kitchen, bath with sink, stool and shower, and a nice large workroom. We shared a bedroom with two single beds. I moved my worktable and Cashibo materials into the workroom to begin study of this difficult language. First, I took the English format of the Aguaruna lessons that Mildred Larson had prepared and, with Olive's help, set up similar lessons in Cashibo. Cashibo-Cacataibo language was similar to Japanese in that a modal word occurred in second position at the beginning of the sentence. Various words had suffixes that had to be matched with whether the verb was transitive or intransitive. That was a verb-final language, with the verb normally occurring at the end of the sentence.

One night at Olive's house, I was awakened by her cries of "Oh! Ouch!" She turned on the light, and we saw that a mass of army ants was moving through the bedroom and they had invaded her bed. At first we tried killing some of them, but we later learned that when army ants come through eating bugs and crumbs, you get out of their way and they will pass on out of the house. That is exactly what they did.

Another night I rose from bed and went into the bathroom to use the restroom. There was a ceiling light with a long string hanging down to turn on the light. At the end of the string was a small metal piece. I pulled the string to turn on the light and then sat down on the commode. Looking sleepy-eyed back at the light string, I saw a small green frog swinging from the end of the string. It had mistaken that small piece of metal for a bug and swallowed it. I called to Olive to bring some scissors with which I cut the string and carried the frog outside, leaving it to somehow get rid of that metal "bug" in its throat.

On January second, my work with the tribal people began in earnest. I helped the Cashibo-Cacataibo bilingual teachers with their studies in their training during their vacation period, January through March. They were being educated through primary school grades, sometimes being just a year or two ahead of their students in those early years of the system. Then they would teach April through December in their communities. At Yarinacocha, they were studying along with bilingual teachers from many other tribes. I helped them with their studies in Spanish while I was also learning more of their language. The three Cashibo-Cacataibo teachers were Gregorio Estrella Odicio from downriver Aguaytia River at Shambuyacu, Juan Chavez Muquini from upriver Aguaytia at Pintayo, and Alfonso Perez Flores from the San Alejandro River where the people spoke with the slightly different Cacataibo dialect.

Toward the end of their training courses in March, one Sunday the Bible lesson was from the book of Acts of the Apostles. I played my accordion for singing several songs in the Native American language. That evening at ten o'clock, teacher Alfonso's wife Carmela came to our house saying that Alfonso had beaten her and his sister and chased them out of their house. I went over there to counsel with him and encouraged the women to sleep in their house. The next day, speaking Spanish, I admonished Alfonso not to beat his wife and sisters.

Another day, I made a trip into Pucallpa, the nearby city, with teacher Juan Chavez' sister to see if there was whooping cough where she lived. We had a horribly rough ride on the back of a large truck. Arriving in Pucallpa, we walked down a back street full of hog wallows to the door of a little hovel. A small boy in the home did have what his mother said was whooping cough. He needed an injection, but they had no money to pay for it in Pucallpa. We suggested that they go to get an injection in the clinic at Yarinacocha.

During the bilingual school teacher training courses, we had study every night Monday through Friday. Monday through Wednesday morning classes for the bilingual teachers were about how to teach Spanish courses. Thursday and Friday morning classes were about how to teach in their native language in the bilingual school. During the daytime, I was working on primers for teaching writing in the native language. Later in the course, the teachers did practice teaching and I gave them suggestions and help. I also worked on monthly plans for their teaching.

One Sunday, only Gregorio, Alfonso's wife Carmela with his sister Sofia, and two little boys came to Sunday morning meeting, but we had a good time discussing Scripture. Toward the end of the teacher training courses, pilot Ralph Borthwick and his wife had a party for all the bilingual teachers and their families, a total of seventy-eight Indians present. Sylvester Dirks gave a good simple Bible message in Spanish.

The Indian school *clausura* (closing exercises) took place on Saturday, March 22. Several Peruvian Department of Education officials came from Lima. The school buildings were all decorated with palm leaves and flags for the occasion. The officials walked between two rows of Indian teachers lining the walk. The planned program proceeded smoothly. Dr. Efraim Morote Best gave a long summary of the activities of the course. During the program a heavy tropical downpour occurred, soaking many people who were not under cover. The noon meal was in the form of a tea for the officials, and the tropical rainfall continued all afternoon. In the evening, the teachers from various tribes gave puppet shows of their native stories.

After the bilingual teacher training school was over, there was a Pano language family conference. Cashibo (Vampire Bat People)-Cacataibo is a member of that family of languages, including Shipibo (Marmoset Monkey People), Capanahua (Rabbit Enemies), Yaminahua (Metal Enemies), and Amahuaca, all in Peru. The conference was a wonderful introduction to the language family to which Cashibo-Cacataibo belonged.

Olive Shell left Yarinacocha to go to the University of Pennsylvania to earn her Ph.D. in linguistics. Her dissertation was a comparative study of the many Panoan languages with reconstruction of proto-Panoan, the mother language of the Panoan sister languages. Thus, she was never in the Cashibo-Cacataibo tribe with me.

In August of 1958, 24-year-old Antonio Mayo Bariria came to the base at Yarinacocha to work with me on the tribal language. He was from Mariscal Caceres on the Lower Aguaytia. I tape-recorded some simple texts about the work of the men, such as gardening, building huts, and making bows and arrows. Also, he recorded descriptions of the work of the women in child care and cooking. During the time I was working with Antonio to translate the stories into Spanish, I received a message from my family in the United States that my grandfather, Roy Caldwell, had died in Macomb, Illinois. He had been a farmer, mechanic, carpenter, and a preacher.

I shed tears and explained to Antonio what had happened. It was not possible for me to go to the States for the funeral.

Later, when I was in the tribe, Antonio's mother told me that a few years previous, her oldest son had died at only about 25 years old. They put his best clothes, including shoes, on him and buried him lying in a canoe cut to his body length. After he was buried, they heard a "tap, tap, tap" sound. It was his shoes pounding on the canoe bottom (there was no embalming). He had not been dead, but only in a coma, from which he awoke under the ground. But the tribal rule was that no one should be dug up after being buried. The mother grieved about this the rest of her life.

# CHAPTER 16: OUR FIRST TRIP TO THE TRIBE

My partner, Irma Schaal, had been working in the finance office at Yarinacocha base while waiting for me to finish my trips to the Shapra and Aguaruna tribes. She had taken time to go to the Aguaruna tribe, traveling with Jeanne Grover while I stayed at Nazaret with Mildred Larson. Finally, the time came that we were both free to make our first trip out to the Aguaytia River. We were limited on the weight of our supplies, as usual, when flying out in the single-engine Aeronca plane. We packed our equipment, had it loaded into the plane, then said our goodbyes to friends at the base. We flew west the one hundred miles over the rain forest to the small Shambuyacu River which flowed into the larger Aguaytia River. Olive Shell and Gloria Gray had lived there with the Cashibo years before. We landed on the small river, but were surprised to see that there was no one there to greet us—only a bull and some cows. The pilot was running late and would just make it back to Yarinacocha close to six o'clock, the deadline for flying in the rain forest to unlighted air strips. So he left us alone in this uninhabited area. A lone, empty, thatch-roofed hut was our only place to stay. We carried our duffel bags and all the equipment to the forlorn hut. As the bull and cows seemed to be wild, we hurriedly carried the boxes inside. There was only one large palm bark shelf about thigh high, but with plenty of room for both our air mattresses and sleeping bags as well as the boxes of food and equipment. The earthen floor did not look very clean, to say the least. There was a door to the hut that we closed as tightly as possible, for, as the sun sank lower toward setting, the cows gathered outside next to the palm bark siding. We had seen one man from a distance, but he disappeared, and we were alone with the cattle for the night. The cows had been given to the tribal leaders at Yarinacocha where a WBT/SIL man raised cattle and chickens to give to tribesmen to help them have meat when wildlife for hunting was scarce. The cows invaded the

*Eight Years in the Amazon Headwaters*

people's gardens, so they just moved away from them and left one man to herd them each day.

The next day dawned, and we were awake early. We hoped that some people would show up soon. To communicate with them in their language, I knew only the main greetings, some medical vocabulary, and questions about their families--and Irma knew less than that. There was much of the language to be learned. The bilingual school teacher, Gregorio Estrella Odicio, knew Spanish quite well because he had spent two years in the Peruvian army in Lima. Thus, with his help we could learn the language faster. But where were he and the people living?

We saw that the cattle had moved away from the hut, so we hurriedly ran to the river to get a container full of water. It would have to be boiled, but first we would need to find some firewood. I had a trusty machete which my Dad had bought for me in Houston, an all-purpose implement for digging holes when we went into the jungle to defecate, for peeling manioc roots, for cutting up small pieces of firewood, and many other uses. We managed to fix a little breakfast. Soon after that, a few Cashibo men arrived. They seemed surprised to find us at Shambuyacu River but told us we could walk over to the Aguaytia River so that a canoe would pick up our belongings. They would be transported to the mouth of the Shambuyacu River, then upriver for a short distance to the settlement on the Aguaytia River. We chose a few things to carry overland, mainly purses and cameras. We followed the men on a nice, rather wide trail over hill and dale about two hours' hike to the settlement. The forest echoed with bird calls and monkey cries. We didn't converse much as we walked, walking quietly. Mexico boot camp training for hiking came in handy.

Arriving at the Aguaytia River, we were met by men, women, and children, and we immediately put to use all the Cashibo language we had learned. After we greeted all the people, teacher Gregorio found a place for us to live on that Saturday morning when he didn't have to teach. Most of the people were gone to a fiesta and others were away working. The house to which we were assigned belonged to a family who had gone to the fiesta. We wondered what they would think about our living in their house, but Gregorio told us to go ahead and move in there.

That morning we had to walk back to Shambuyacu accompanied by two little boys and a little girl. All the way over there we were nervous, anticipating meeting that wild bull again. When we arrived, he was lying down and never moved until Greg arrived back to Shambuyacu. Finally, on Sunday morning, we joyfully packed up our belongings again. Irma lost weight because she couldn't eat or sleep surrounded by the cattle. All our equipment was packed into the canoe. We didn't think it would take very long to travel downriver to the mouth of the Shambuyacu River, then upriver on the larger Aguaytia River to the Cashibo settlement. But the men fished for supper on the way and we didn't arrive until four o'clock in the afternoon. We were famished even though we had been given an egg, a plantain, and a piece of papaya fruit to eat. Fortunately, we had taken boiled water with us. After we arrived, the men unloaded our belongings and placed them in our house. We unpacked our cooking equipment, set it up, and ate a hearty meal. Afterward, we bathed in the beautifully clear Aguaytia River. It was dry season.

We tried to start our generator so we would be ready to make radio contact with Yarinacocha base, but we couldn't start the motor. We had four days to get it started. If they didn't hear from us by then, they would send a plane out to check on us. We felt we couldn't afford a flight so soon, so we prayed for wisdom and tried to get it to work. The Lord answered our prayer in an unexpected way. Two *mestizo* young men who were employed by the Peruvian government came through to spray the houses with DDT insecticide. We asked them if they could start the generator, and, sure enough, they did. Were we happy! We rejoiced so many times, knowing we were under God's protection. Living wasn't easy, but we were comfortable and well situated, ready to go to work learning the language.

The women were really friendly and sweet to us. They were anxious for us to learn the language and were extremely helpful. We had all the material to work with that Olive prepared, so it wasn't nearly as difficult as it might have been. Many times we rejoiced over God's leading. Previous observation and activity with others who were more experienced, such as we did with Millie and Jeanne in the Aguaruna tribe, were vital background before going to our own tribe. Even so, the languages and cultures were completely different.

Our hut was a split-level design. Under one-half of the thatched roof was the dirt floor. Above that space was the loft, my bedroom. Under the other half on a raised, palm-bark floor was the kitchen and Irma's bed. The rooms were about 8 feet by 10 feet with cane-pole walls and no door on the one doorway to the outside. From the dirt floor to the palm-bark floor was a "stairway," a big, slanted log with three notches in it. The notches were made for small, bare feet, and our larger feet with sneakers barely fit sideways in them. In time, we became agile at going up and down the "stairs." Access to my loft was a sturdy ladder made of two, long poles with pole rungs, fastened by vines.

The whole house was rather wobbly. Sleeping in the loft, I felt like the baby in the song "Rock-a-bye baby, in the tree top". My folding table, two folding aluminum chairs, and two folding cots were most of our furniture. We scouted around and found a small, flat board to which we tied some legs to make a workbench. We found a piece of balsa log and put nails in it to hang up utensils. We improvised another platform for pans, radio, and books. At Yarinacocha I had a little cupboard made with a tightly closed door to keep the dishes bugproof. It also had a silverware drawer in the bottom. With all these conveniences, we felt pretty modern. We cooked on a Primus pressure burner, but we boiled our water over a wood fire on the ground-level, dirt-floor patio. One of the boys was hired to carry water from the river and to build the fires for us. One day a woman brought us a great big fish wrapped in banana leaves and cooked over her coals. We had fish chowder for supper, using powdered milk with a little flour we had brought. The native women also brought us eggs, avocado, papaya, and bananas.

On school days we took turns monitoring the bilingual school for about half a day each day. The rest of the day was spent learning the language. We were becoming fairly fluent in the language by hearing the language all around us and interacting with the people. Irma didn't know one word of Cashibo when she came, so she was progressing exceptionally well in speaking and understanding the Cashibo-Cacataibo language.

Irma Schall in one of the houses provided by the Cashibo-Cacataibo

On a typical day we would get up about 5:30 a.m., dress, prepare and eat breakfast by 6:30 a.m., and finish washing and drying dishes by 7 a.m. Irma made breakfast and dinner and I prepared noon lunch for one week and the next week we reversed the schedule. The one who did not cook would wash and dry the dishes. After eating, we would do what we wanted for about an hour—read, write letters, or pray. Then we went visiting for language practice, went to check on the school, or stayed in our hut and studied the language material we had. When we went visiting, we looked over the scene and made up conversation about what they were doing. It was very simple conversation at first, but the Native Americans were very gracious. They were patient and when we said something wrong, they told us the right way and continued correcting us until we said it right. At noon we ate lunch and took a siesta Latin style, though the Indians didn't lie down in the daytime unless they were ill. Then we studied, visited some more, or did medical work. About three or four o'clock we bathed, then prepared supper to eat around five o'clock. The evening was spent talking and studying, then listening to the battery-powered short-wave radio. These activities were subject to interruptions by the people.

Cashibo women wore handmade skirts or dresses of the simplest style. Material was sewn into a sack-like design. Nursing women sometimes wore only a skirt. The skirts were usually made of hand-spun cotton thread, also woven by hand, a very strong, durable cloth.

Language study took effort, planning, and energy. One had to think quickly to form sentences used for conversation, then concentrate on understanding their answer.

One morning we discovered that a couple of boys had been stealing some of our belongings. They had reached in through the wall and taken medical syringes and needles for giving injections. At that time, we re-used the same ones over and over by sterilizing them between uses. They also had stolen laxatives, amoeba medicine and other pills. We told teacher Gregorio immediately. After intense discussion, we convinced the boys that they should bring back what they had stolen, though they only brought a few at a time. They had eaten a number of laxative pills and amoeba medications. The teacher said they do not have respect for their fathers and adults like the children did in the old days.

Our medical cases were of various types at that time. A little girl had some kind of infection on her foot, possibly of fungus origin. Gregorio's wife, Delfina, had a fish bone in her throat that had become infected. Both of these infections were treated with penicillin and healed. One man had a case of gonorrhea that we also treated with penicillin.

Delfina was a friendly woman. She had been the young wife of deceased Chief Bolivar, but was given to Gregorio when her elderly husband died. Delfina had a daughter by the chief and two sons, Carlos and Jorge, by Gregorio. Chief Bolivar had been well-known for his friendship with Spanish-speaking engineers who planned the route of the trans-Andean road into the rain forest extending from Lima to Pucallpa. Bolivar showed the engineers the best place to put the suspension bridge crossing the Aguaytia River. Many Cashibo men worked on the road. Delfina had the privilege of traveling by car with Bolivar over the Andes Mountains to Lima. It was a frightful trip for someone only used to living in the rain forest. Bolivar was disliked by the upper Aguaytia people who were given the choice of either going along with the white men or being shot. Many of them died for wanting to keep their old culture. German anthropologist Günther Tessmann did field work among the Cashibo-Cacataibo in the 1920's. Even at that early time, he realized that before long, white men would be impacting the native culture with many changes.

One Friday was Labor Day in Peru. We helped the teacher prepare a program. He gave a speech for about one and one-half hours with a song now and then and a poem by one of the students who repeated after the teacher in Spanish. Three of the children did a dance as an example of Cashibo-Cacataibo dances in the olden days.

The people of this tribe were both hunters and gatherers as well as horticulturalists, having small gardens raising plantain, bananas, sweet potatoes, papayas, manioc, and potatoes of various kinds. They were especially well-known for domesticating wild animals and birds. They domesticated small tapirs, as told in their myths that their demigod Incas taught them to do. The young tapirs would be fed by the Cashibo and, as they grew older, would go out into the wild to feed during the daytime and return to their human owners during the evening to spend the night. It made the people very angry when white men would come into the area and kill their tame tapirs as they fed in the wild.

Aside from tapirs, wild hogs (*javalinas*) were also tamed. One older woman had a baby hog that she even nursed at her breast. Another woman had a large, black pet spider monkey that stood waist high on two legs. She cried bitterly when the elders of the settlement decided that her pet must be killed for the people to eat. The spider monkey reminded me of a human teen-ager, full of personality and generally good humored. The owner of a pet never ate the meat of their pet.

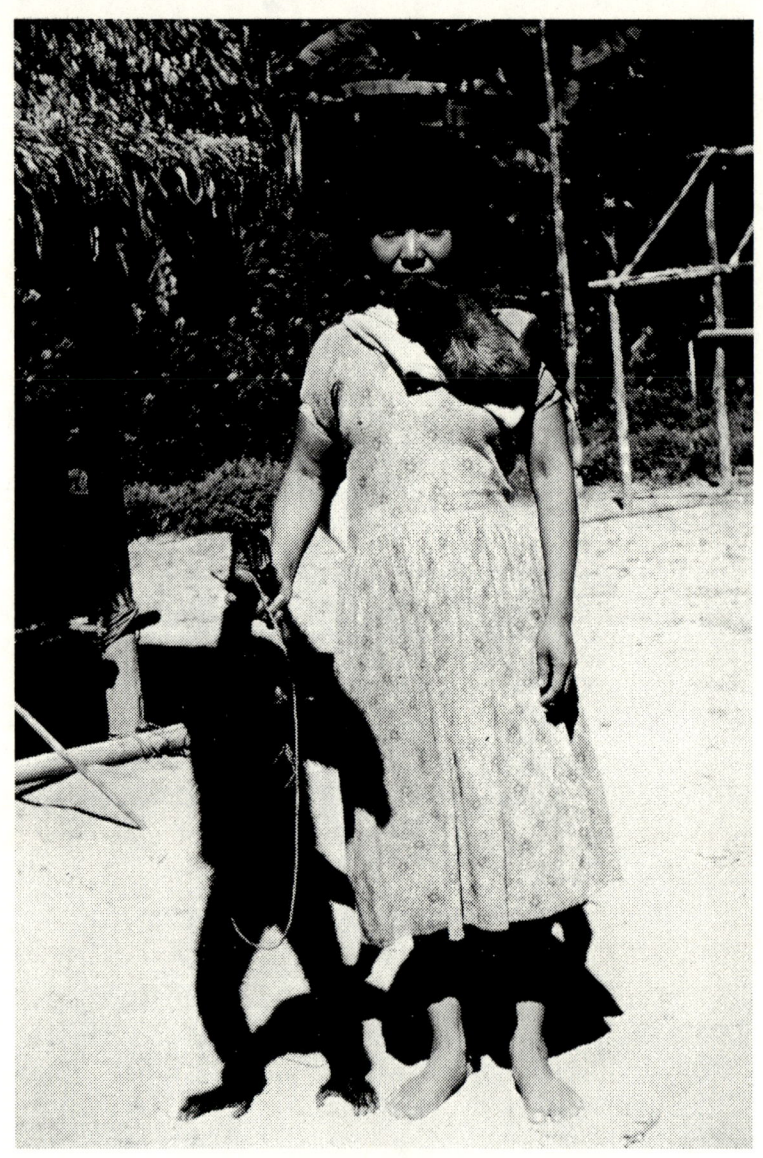

Cashibo woman with young howler monkey
on her shoulder and pet spider monkey

Marmoset monkeys are very small monkeys about six or eight inches long, but very smart. One family had a marmoset monkey that they tried to keep tied, but it continually kept untying the little knots of the rope. One time I was typing some language material on my portable typewriter when the marmoset monkey got loose and came to sit on my typewriter. The monkey was intrigued by the machine, so much so that I couldn't type. Then it climbed onto my shoulder. Finally, the owners retrieved the cute animal and tied it up once again.

The howler monkey was a reddish brown-haired animal that whined. The ones I saw as pets had bad personalities. In the wild, adults were able to howl so loudly that it could be heard five miles away, particularly when a whole group of them was howling at once. Even so, as a pet it was greatly loved by its owner.

A South American cousin to the North American raccoon is the ring-tailed coati, called a *sisi* in Cashibo. The coati doesn't like to be tied and tries to bite people who come near. This is one animal that is edible and I was always glad when they brought us one for dinner.

# CHAPTER 17: UPRIVER ON THE AGUAYTIA

    We stayed with the downriver people about three months and decided to go upriver past Aguaytia town toward the headwaters. On our river trips, we learned to drape a towel from our head to shield our bodies from the bright reflection of the tropical sun on the river water. Previously, I had worn a jungle helmet that only kept the sun off my head and face but gave no protection for the arms and lower body. As the sun would move from east to west, we would move the towel from one side to the other. To travel upriver, we went south since in South America the rivers flow north, the opposite of our Mississippi River's southward flow.

    As our canoe was paddled upriver, we passed the settlement of another group of Cashibo-Cacataibo who were the direct descendents of the deceased Chief Bolivar. Also, east of the Aguaytia River was the farm of a former North American missionary, Mr. Reifsnyder, who lived with his wife and daughter. Their son was grown and had left home to serve in the armed forces of the United States. Mr. Reifsnyder raised cattle on his ranch and spent some time in Lima, the capital city. From the village it was about fifteen or twenty miles up to the town of Aguaytia. The town had a large port area so that trucks from Lima could back down to the edge of the river to load up bananas and plantain which were bought by the thousands right off the canoes. These were then transported over the Andes Mountains to Lima. Some buildings in the town of Aguaytia had metal roofs, some tile, and some palm-thatched roofs. A few buildings stood high on the hills, safe from any floods when the river was high.

Aguaytia bridge and location of the town of Aguaytia (or Puente Aguaytia)

Irma and I walked up the hill to a restaurant which looked promising. We ordered a typical Peruvian meal with fried plantain, manioc, and *lomo saltado*, a type of fried beef strips cooked with tomatoes and onions. Sitting in the restaurant while we were waiting for the food to be cooked, we looked above us. There was no ceiling—just rafters and a thatched roof. But on the rafters there were big, healthy rats running around. We almost lost our appetites, but the meal served was very tasty.

On a later trip to "the bridge", so named for the suspension bridge, which at that time was the largest suspension bridge in South America, we ate at a restaurant down by the river. We each ordered a dish of rice with small pieces of meat in it. After we went upriver, the Native Americans asked us where we had eaten at the bridge. We explained to them where it was, and they said, "Oh, we never eat there. The little pieces of meat in the rice are rat meat."

When the Cashibo were at the bridge, they whispered when they spoke in their own language in the town. They were ashamed to speak it, so at that time most of the men spoke just enough Spanish to buy and sell goods. Since they have had the bilingual schools for many years, now the younger generations speak more Spanish.

We made acquaintance with the policeman at Aguaytia town. He was also in the army since policemen in Peru are in their national military. On a later trip to the bridge from upriver, my machete was stolen. I explained to him that it had been given to me by my father and had my initials L.W. on it. I didn't think there was any chance that he would find it, but later he actually found it and gave it back to me.

At the bridge, we met some Indians from upriver, so we transferred our goods from the downriver canoe to an upriver one. We set out on the trip upriver that is also uphill. When the water is low, there are over sixty sets of rapids we traveled through against the current to reach the settlements. It was dry season, which is like North American summer. The river was low, with many rocky beaches exposed. Approaching white-water rapids, we would get out of the canoe to walk on the beach so the men wouldn't have to push our body weight up against the strong current. We wore our sneakers through water and over rocky beaches. Usually a pair of sneakers lasted only about three months. In all three tribes, the people didn't like for women to wear slacks, so we only wore skirts and blouses or dresses. Also, they didn't want to see women's knees or above.

Pushing the canoe upriver through the rapids

The river would have rapids, then a long, deep section, then more rapids in shallow water. We were periodically getting out of the canoe for the rapids and climbing back into the canoe for the deep water. In dry season, the still water would be crystal clear so one could see deep into the river. Large sting rays about thirty-five inches in diameter were one danger in the river, along with two kinds of caiman. There are black caiman and white caiman, one edible and the other not edible to the Indians. There were no anacondas in the fast-flowing water in the foothills of the Andes Mountains, but there were other deadly poisonous snakes. We were often walking on a path with tall weeds on both sides. I wondered if we might step on a snake. One time a group of five or six of us were walking to visit another Indian location. All of a sudden I saw a snake slither across the path between two barefoot boys in front of me.

Like the Aguaruna, the Cashibo-Cacataibo usually had small, thatch-roof lean-tos in which to have shelter from storms or to camp in overnight at distant locations. Sometimes there would be rain in the higher mountains (five thousand foot *Cordillera Azul* or Blue Ridge to the west) which would make the Aguaytia River rise to fifteen feet within hours. There were a few *mestizo* farmers who spoke only Spanish living along the Aguaytia above the bridge, but farther upriver toward the headwaters there were only Native Americans.

The Pintayo location where Olive and Gloria stayed with the Indians had been abandoned. The people had moved upriver a short distance. We arrived there and were assigned a hut in which to live on the bank of the river in a clearing with a few other huts. Our only privacy was the mosquito nets in which we slept. The net I brought from Texas was a "see through" net which made it so that I needed to get up before dawn to dress in the mosquito net. Later, after we returned to Yarinacocha base, we both had heavy unbleached muslin mosquito nets made which gave us complete privacy inside for dressing.

Our little hut with a hole covered with plastic in the roof

   Again, one of the first things we did was to hire a young person to bring our water from the river and to make fires to boil our drinking water. We also hired a woman to wash our clothes in the river. Pay was in the form of trade goods instead of money: items such as needles, thread, and matches for the women; and fish line, fish hooks, and flashlight batteries for the boys. Sometime later, we brought used clothing, which was good if it was heavy cloth but not good if it was rayon which didn't last through rough washings in the river. One waterboy received a nice, North American-made maroon corduroy shirt in payment for keeping us supplied with boiled drinking water. He wore it day after day. Three months later when we came back from Yarinacocha, he was still wearing it. I asked, "Have you washed it?" "No," he answered, "I was afraid it would lose its color." At that time, Peruvian cloth sold in the rain forest faded when you washed it. I told him his shirt would not fade, so he finally washed it.
   One day a man had not returned from his garden upriver, and everyone was concerned about him. So we set out walking uphill and downhill on a narrow, grassy trail to try to find him. Finally, we arrived to where he was and found that he had been snake-bitten

by a poisonous snake. Someone had brought a canoe upriver to transport him back home. By that time, it was getting dark. Irma and I had brought our kerosene lantern that was lifted and held out in front of the canoe to see where the current was. We arrived back at the settlement, and the Indians gave him a mixture of kerosene and water to drink. They placed him on a pallet in a hut, digging a hole in the dirt floor for him to use as a toilet. Slowly, he began to improve and the swelling went down. He survived the poisonous snakebite.

One morning at dawn, we were awakened by a man shouting repeatedly, though we were not close enough to hear what he was saying. We dressed and went over to see that a man was lying out in the open, shouting and raising his hands into the air. The people said that the evil spirits were bothering him. In his language he was saying, "Go away! Leave me alone!" Not knowing well enough how to pray in the Cashibo-Cacataibo language yet, Irma and I each prayed in English (which no Native American understood), saying, "In the name of Jesus Christ, we command you evil spirits to go away and leave this man alone! By the power of the one true God, we command you to go!" Just after we prayed and opened our eyes, the man sat up and said in Cashibo, "They have left me now. They are gone!" We praised God for answering our prayers.

We had to cook over a fire on the ground, eating mostly the foods that the people ate from their gardens: bananas, plantain, sweet potatoes, potatoes, papaya, and avocados. When the avocados were in season there were so many of them that we ate avocado three meals a day. To obtain wild meat, we would give one cartridge to a good hunter, and he would hunt for deer, wild hogs (*javalina*), or wild birds of various kinds. Usually with one shot, a good hunter brought back a leg and thigh of the animal for us and he would divide the rest of the meat with the people in the clearing. A few years later, a good hunter asked us to change our policy to giving two cartridges to hunt with, one for killing the animal and one for defending the hunter, especially among the wild hogs which would charge him. These men used twelve and sixteen gauge shotguns. There were only a few older men who still hunted with large bows and seven-foot arrows.

I had a reel-to-reel recorder that was powered by a Briggs and Stratton motor used also to generate power for the radio contacts with the base. Some of the older men came to record myths, histories, and folklore. This was needed to study the narrative forms of the language in preparation for Bible translation, as well as for us to learn vocabulary and historical background, including beliefs of the people. We also carried pencils and notebooks in our pockets to be able to write down new words that we would hear and our guesses as to their meanings. Some of these guesses were correct, but others were corrected by checking with a language consultant.

Teacher Juan Chavez Muquini lived farther upriver. It was there that he held his bilingual school classes. At a later time we went to his location and found that the books were all still in boxes and he was not teaching classes at all. I informed the director at Yarinacocha base about the abandoned school who said that Juan would have to be dismissed as a teacher. He was still collecting salary from the Department of Education. We would have to train and appoint a new teacher. Juan Chavez had a fairly good command of the Spanish language and had leadership qualities, so we were sorry that he would not be teaching. We later found a young man named Tito who was trained at Yarinacocha in the bilingual school teacher training course and began teaching the following year.

We didn't stay upriver long but became acquainted with the people and collected some recordings. When we left for the bridge in a large canoe, it was a beautiful, clear day. However, after the first half-hour, a storm suddenly brewed, and we had a torrential tropical downpour. We couldn't see where we were going, but the men poling and steering the canoe were very experienced and knew the river well. Our raincoats were not much help, but we went through the ritual of wearing them anyway. The storm was soon over, and the rest of the trip was beautiful weather. We stopped right outside the town of Aguaytia and changed to clean clothes. We decided to leave half of our equipment upriver because the next time we would go there first. We paid two boys to take care of the equipment we left.

# CHAPTER 18: TRIP TO THE SAN ALEJANDRO RIVER

Mr. Reifsnyder met us at Puente (bridge) Aguaytia and drove us east on the gravel road to a place where he left his truck behind. We changed to muleback transportation for the trip five miles off the main road to the Reifsnyders' home. We had taken longer than expected to finish our business in Aguaytia, so that when we arrived at the turnoff and had the mules saddled and ready to ride, it was five o'clock in the afternoon. We had no idea how long it would take to arrive at his farm. Neither one of us had much previous experience riding horses, much less mules. By seven o'clock it was pitch black, a bad storm was beginning, and we couldn't see any sign of a house. We rode over very high hills, through creeks, and across high, forested areas. We could see Mr. Reifsnyder only when lightning flashed. Finally, he took out his flashlight so that we could follow him. The wind began to blow and the rain came in torrents. The stubborn mules insisted on turning their backs to the rain and didn't want to budge. The pack mule led us off the trail and we wandered in the valley. Mr. Reifsnyder finally caught the mule and led it back to the path. At last we came to his fields and cow pastures. We arrived at the Reifsnyder home at 7:30 p.m., cold, wet, and weary. After introductions and a short visit with his wife and daughter, we were shown to our room where we quickly changed to our bedclothes and went to bed. We had a lovely stay there on Sunday in their native-style house with earthen floor but furnished with comfortable furniture.

Monday morning we rode the mules back to the main road on a nice, sunny day. We became brave and both galloped those mules. It was fun once we were used to them. The mules were the size of small horses, more like ponies. Mr. Reifsnyder had 750 to 800 acres and 200 head of beef cattle plus milk cows, chickens, dogs, cats, and a fruit orchard. Arriving at the main road, we waited for a truck, just any commercial truck hauling produce. We waited from 10:30 a.m. until 12:30 p.m. The first truck that came picked us up with all our baggage. We traveled twenty miles per hour down the hilly, rough road for two hours until we came to the home of a missionary couple, the Louis Rankins. They were independent missionaries working with Spanish-speaking Peruvians. Mrs. Rankin, as a fifty-year-old widow, had gone to Peru and studied Spanish in Irma's class in Lima. She then went to work at the Reifsnyder farm. There she met Mr. Rankin, a bachelor of fifty-five years old. They fell in love and were married about a year previous. They were crazy about one another. Louis Rankin was a Dallas Theological Seminary graduate who knew both Hebrew and Greek. His main attraction for the local people living along the road was that he did dental work in this area where there were no other dentists for miles. The people were also attracted to the gospel and some had become evangelicals. The Rankins were in the process of building a new home there where they lived, located eighty miles west of Pucallpa. Since they temporarily had only a small aluminum roof under which to live, they made a bed for us in their Volkswagen and it worked out fine.

We had written and sent a letter to teacher Alfonso Perez Flores that we would be in San Alejandro town (with the same name as the river) on the third or fourth of November. The Cacataibo were to come downriver to pick us up and take us to their location upriver. When we arrived at the town on November 4, the Cacataibo had already been there and left. The main road follows the river for a little distance, so we raced out in the Volkswagen to a location where we could take a trail in a twenty-minute walk to an upriver location. When we arrived at the riverbank, we were told the Cacataibo had passed two hours earlier, and we had missed them. We couldn't get anyone else to take us upriver, so we went back home with Mr. Rankin and stayed with them until Saturday afternoon. We had sent word upriver for the Cacataibo to return on Saturday and pick us up, but when we arrived on that day they were not there again. We had no assurance that they had received our message. But with Mr. Rankin's help, we made a deal with a Peruvian couple to take us upriver. We stayed overnight in the home of an evangelical Peruvian family in the little town of San Alejandro. The next morning the couple said they couldn't take us because they didn't have anyone else to help and our load was too heavy for them to handle. As a result, we began our wait to see if the Indians would come. Finally they arrived on Monday morning. That was one of the longest weekends we have ever spent. The wife in the evangelical home was a good hostess and prepared all our meals, which were very tasty.

In San Alejandro, there were no sanitary facilities in the homes. However, this family had an outhouse. It was situated over a little spring that flowed downhill into the river. Behind the "Johnny", there were two pigs fenced in which fought over the waste products directly below even while a person was sitting in the outhouse. Everyone bathed in the river and most people drank the river water, with great possibilities of disease.

On the morning of December eighth, our belongings finally were loaded into a canoe and we started up the San Alejandro River at about one o'clock. That river was a very slow and muddy river. Going upstream, you could sit still and not be carried back by the current. It doesn't have the swift current that the Aguaytia River had. The river began to rise that day, therefore we stopped about 4:00 p.m. at an empty hut and spent the night there. There were actually two huts, one for us and one for the Cacataibo men. The river had risen about six feet that afternoon, making it too deep to pole. Very frequently, the Cacataibo men had to stop to smoke their homemade pipes. They bought their tobacco in the town of San Alejandro. Even the little eleven and twelve year olds smoked. The next morning after a quick breakfast, we set out on our trip upriver at seven o'clock and arrived there at one o'clock. We spent five days at this school site. We had brought only the bare minimum of supplies, including medicines. Teacher Alfonso, his wife, and children invited us to stay in their home. Their hut was not yet completed in this fairly new location. One night we had a terrific windstorm, and the rain blew into the house. We tried to cover our beds with plastic but the wind blew it right off. To say the least, we spent a sleepless night in wet beds.

At that time, there was an epidemic of diarrhea and vomiting in that area. Two *mestizo* babies had diarrhea, so we treated them and they recovered well. The *mestizos* asked us to go upriver to see another sick baby, which we did, and left medicine for diarrhea, but we had no medication for vomiting. The next day they brought the baby down to us, but it died very soon. That was the first person Irma had seen dying. The baby was the only child of a young couple. They were really broken hearted about losing their nine-month-old baby. Irma and I also cried. The *mestizo* couple had come across an old copy of a Spanish-language Bible with the cover missing. They didn't even know it was a Bible but had been reading it, saying it was very interesting. We read some comforting verses to them and also explained the way of salvation. I marked Bible verses for them to read. They seemed to accept the death of the baby as God's will and to be resigned to it when they finally left.

On Sunday, December 13, we started downriver, arriving at the town of San Alejandro about five o'clock in the late afternoon. We stayed again in the home of the Christian family who had been our host and hostess before. Mr. Rankin picked us up and drove us back to Yarinacocha base. We made the eighty-mile trip in three hours which was really record time for that unpaved road. The road wasn't muddy since it had not rained for some time. It was not quite as exciting to arrive back at the base via Volkswagen as it would have been by plane, but it surely was cheaper. We took a nice vacation in Lima, then were assigned different jobs at the base until we returned to the tribe.

# *CHAPTER 19: SECOND TRIP TO THE AGUAYTIA RIVER*

On May 3, 1959, Irma and I left the Yarinacocha base in the afternoon in a Helio Courier float plane, a plane which can take off and land on short strips. That year we were able to land on the lower Aguaytia River right where Gregorio had his school. We were met by all the Indians at that location, all eager to see us. Gregorio did not have a hut for us at his location, however, we were taken to another location, a fifteen minute walk by trail downriver. This meant that we would have to walk that fifteen minutes every day to visit the bilingual school, good exercise for us. The men took our equipment by canoe down to where we would stay.

Another house style on the Lower Aguaytia River

The thatch-roof hut in which we lived had a palm-bark wall on half of one side and a piece of screening up on the other end. Our bedroom for our two air mattresses and sleeping bags was in the room with walls. There was one partition right in the center across the room that separated our bedroom from the kitchen. The size of the hut was nine feet by fourteen feet. We didn't bring our aluminum cots nor our folding table this time, so we were sleeping with our air mattresses right on the palm bark floor. An older woman named Rara (Clara in English or Spanish) graciously gave us a small table and bench to use. We improvised another bench for our Primus pressure burner, made of two boards held up by two metal, two-foot high cans in which crackers were packed. There were shelves all around the kitchen but quite high up. We kept our small supply of canned food and jars up there in cardboard boxes like a cupboard. We were really quite comfortable, and so happy we didn't have to live where the cattle were.

Rara weaving a basket

There was a beautiful, little spring up behind the houses about a two-minute walk away. We drew our water from there, boiling it of course, and we also bathed there. The water was clear and cold. The river was still high from rainy season and also very muddy, making us especially thankful for the little spring. The people said they didn't have any manioc because the pigs had eaten it all and ravaged their gardens. They did bring us some papayas, lemons, and bananas that we enjoyed.

When repacking at Yarinacocha due to our cargo being overweight for the airplane, Irma removed a pair of sneakers to lighten the load. In the tribe, she began to put on her pair of shoes and discovered that they were both for the left foot. All she had to wear was a good pair that she wanted to preserve for wearing in the town of Aguaytia. We also discovered that we had brought no matches with us. The Native Americans gave us a box of matches to help. When two Indian young men from that location went upriver to the town of Aguaytia, Irma gave them money to buy her a pair of sneakers. They came back with a pair of boy's high top shoes. She only laced them part way up and they fit fine. Actually, they were much stronger than the kind for girls, and she liked them better.

At that location, there was a total of ten people: two older men, one young man, two older women, one young woman, a little girl, two little boys, and a baby boy. The rest of the people were just fifteen minutes away, but our location was rather quiet and, at times, lonesome. Irma and I had decided to take turns going over to the school to help Gregorio. I went on Monday morning while Irma stayed home to study the Cashibo-Cacataibo language. Between greeting visitors and getting the wash lady started on our wash, she didn't achieve much, but at least she could practice conversing in their language. For conversation practice, Irma felt she needed to go alone to visit as much as possible. She went alone over to the school and that was good language experience for her, also.

Gregorio was doing a good job teaching. His attitude seemed to have improved greatly over the previous year. He seemed to have grasped teaching principles to the point of being able to apply them in his teaching. He was very open to help and had taken our suggestions and applied them. We were very pleased with his work.

We had a sewing class for the women of the area every afternoon they were able to come. I bought some little dresses already cut out that Annabelle Weber at the base had procured in the States. They were given to her because of a mistake made on them in the factory. The women were very anxious to sew the pieces together. They would come by one o'clock and stay until five o'clock, sewing the dresses by hand for their little girls. All the sewing they had done before was without patterns and would look either too loose or too tight. We taught them how to blind stitch and to make different kinds of seams. They were eager to learn and worked intensely even in stressful situations. For example, two of the women had small children who always wanted to nurse, so they sat there nursing their children while sewing. Sometimes the child would cry loudly. Also, we heard a lot of conversation during that time which helped us to learn the language. We didn't understand all of it, but our ears were becoming attuned to the language.

One evening four Shipibo boys came from downriver to tell us their bilingual school teacher was very ill. The Shipibo language is a sister language similar to Cashibo-Cacataibo in the Pano language family. The Shipibo teacher wanted an airplane to come out the next day to take him back to Yarinacocha base. We tried to find out what his symptoms were, but they spoke little Spanish and we knew no Shipibo. Finally, we told them we would talk on the radio with their worker Jim Lauriault at the base. As a result, the plane flew in the next afternoon. Since the plane came so close to our settlement, we had ordered a few items which were delivered. It was great to see pilot Jim and co-pilot George even though they only stayed a few minutes. We were very glad for the opportunity to receive and send out mail. Later, we heard that when they landed the plane at the Shipibo location, they had motor trouble, and it was necessary for them to stay overnight. We were planning to have a flight come out to us the last of the month before going upriver and at that time would have our mail sent by plane instead of over the road through the town of Aguaytia.

Irma suggested that she might go home after Peru branch conference instead of waiting until Christmas because she felt so out of contact with her supporters in the States. She felt that all her personal relationships needed to be renewed. I said I would like to stay until a year from conference in order that someone would occupy the tribe continually. We felt we shouldn't leave the tribe unoccupied due to the lack of occupancy for five years after Gloria was married.

I started to walk to school one morning, and, just as I began walking on the trail, I screamed. Irma was nearby and knew immediately that I had seen a poisonous snake. I was startled when I looked down to see it a step away. If I had not looked down, I would have stepped directly on it. The snakes blend in so well with the environment that it is difficult to see them. The Indians have keen eyes and rarely miss a dangerous situation. We walk the trail over to the school alone, but with some anxiety. At these times, we feel the need to trust in God. He knows we don't have the extra sensory vision and sense of smell that the Indian people have. They can be floating with the current midriver and smell wild hogs back in the woods. That very morning I saw the snake, Irma had been praying to the Lord about the lack of experiences this time in the tribe to make us depend on Him more and feel the need of His presence. When the snake incident took place, her thoughts immediately made her realize how many dangers we escaped and how God protects us each moment.

One Saturday morning, an elderly man about sixty years old named Poloponte came over to see us. He began to tell us about the old days of the people, so we put the reel-to-reel tape on the recorder and recorded his stories. His vocabulary was a little different from the younger generation. The younger Cashibo mix some of their language with Shipibo words or, occasionally, Spanish words. At times they have given us a word for something and later someone would tell us that it was a Shipibo word rather than Cashibo-Cacataibo.

That afternoon we made our last trip to the Shambuyacu River to get the rest of Olive Shell's pans with which to cook. We were thankful that we didn't have to land there in the plane as we did the first trip. The building in which we found shelter the previous year had become a barn for the cattle. The unoccupied huts had fallen down. There were only two families left to take care of the bull and cows. We collected Olive's pans and were happy to leave the bull that didn't like strangers. The trail was muddy and sloppy. We had to cross shallow, narrow streams, and in one place Irma went in the mud over her sneaker tops up to her ankles. She was glad to wash the mud off in the Shambuyacu River and again in the Aguaytia River when we arrived back home. We were tired from the hike and went to bed at eight o'clock in the evening, sleeping until six in the morning. It rained hard from six in the evening off and on all night, but Sunday dawned a beautiful day. The river and the spring were both high and muddy but cleared up quickly since that was the end of rainy season.

Sunday night it rained heavily again all night. There were loud claps of thunder and bright flashes of lightning. The Aguaytia River rose higher than we had seen it. The hut we were in last year was in a dangerous area when the river was so high. The water came to the edge of the hut. The Cashibo location on the Aguaytia River is in the foothills of the Andes where the cool air of the Andes Mountains clashes with the warm air of the lowland rain forest. This causes extreme thunderstorms with downpours of up to twelve feet of rain per year. We were glad that our hut was in a higher location on this second stay in the tribe.

On my birthday, May 12, we had many people visiting along with the sewing class of women, keeping us busy until five o'clock in the afternoon. One visitor was an Indian fellow who Irma had met in Lima on our yearly vacation. He had come out to the tribe to visit his mother and also wanted to see our setup. We had a good visit speaking mostly Cashibo language even though he speaks Spanish well. Usually, if a Native American speaks Spanish, they prefer to do so, but he spoke in Cashibo and did so happily, though we were just learning his language.

After the company left, Irma began baking my birthday cake. We had no oven, so she baked it over an open fire in a heavy black iron skillet. She made half a recipe at a time to make two layers. Since it looked like it might rain again, she had to bake it in Rara*'s* cookhouse because our fire was outside in the open. We had a young teen-ager named Rita working for us to bring wood for the fire and water from the river to boil on the outside fire. When it would rain, she would also use Rara's fire. Irma took an egg, divided the white from the yolk, and beat the white stiff with a fork. Then she boiled a brown sugar mixture and made a seven minute-type frosting. It was a perfect, frosted birthday cake. Supper was quite late, but after supper Irma gave me her gift, the best gift in my life—a khaki wraparound dress which she had the sewing lady make for me at Yarinacocha. I was completely surprised by this wonderful gift which fit perfectly. The khaki fabric was heavy enough for the Indian women to beat on the rocks and it wouldn't fall apart. We had been reading the book *Prince Caspian* by C. S. Lewis, so to celebrate, we read a couple of extra chapters that night.

It had been raining most of the time and was quite chilly. Irma didn't have a sleeping bag with her on this trip—just a blanket. She had some flannel pajamas, but was still not warm. We had some equipment ordered and sent by road from Yarinacocha to Puente Aguaytia. The roads had been so muddy due to the rain that we wondered if it would ever arrive. Even so, it came in less than a week. On Monday morning, a Shipibo man came from Aguaytia town bringing our equipment in his canoe, only the items we had designated to be brought to Lower Aguaytia River. The rest of the equipment sent by road would remain at the bridge (Aguaytia town) until we could pick it up on our way upriver. Irma's two right foot sneakers and her flannel pajamas came, for which she was thankful. Now she had two matching pairs of sneakers.

Wednesday morning was very busy. The women's sewing class, which usually met in the afternoon, was attended in the morning. Antonio Mayo came to work with me on some texts I had been collecting from him at Yarinacocha base. One of Poloponte's wives came with her little girl who had an infected sore on her head. Her mother said that they previously had taken a worm out of it. We scheduled a radio talk with Dr. Eichenberger at the base, and he confirmed the need to give penicillin injections for the infection. I cleaned up the sore, cut the hair off all around it, and gave the first injection, telling them to come back for two more injections on certain days. The little girl screamed, kicked, and flailed while Irma tried to hold her down as I gave her each injection. Of our tribal experiences, Irma liked the medical work least. She felt she had a weak stomach for it, but that experience helped her to get over that feeling. Irma had to leave about ten o'clock to visit Gregorio's adult reading class. All these experiences on one Wednesday morning exhausted us by noon.

Sara, an older woman, brought a large turtle on Thursday morning. We watched her cut it up with an axe and then clean it. It had six hard-shelled eggs in it and five eggs with no shells. It must have been preparing to lay and bury those eggs in the sand. We were given a piece of turtle meat and two of the eggs. We made a stew of the meat adding some vegetables for supper. The next morning, we ate the turtle eggs for breakfast. We decided that we would just as soon not see another turtle egg. After boiling them for five minutes, the yolk was cooked, but the white part looked like mucous. The meat wasn't so bad but the eggs must have required longer cooking—or something.

Irma was cleaning under her air mattress and blanket where there was sand. She put them both out in the sun, where they stayed since she forgot about them. Meanwhile, the sun caused the air in the air mattress to get hot, expand, and burst with a loud bang. We tried patching it to no avail. The fabric had just come apart. She was mortified and even felt like crying. She didn't get much sleep on the hard palm bark floor, so we begrudgingly called by radio for an airplane to bring Irma an air mattress.

We heard on my shortwave radio that a TAPSA commercial airplane had crashed in the rain forest. That is the plane on which we flew into Lima for our vacation. We usually flew on Faucett Airlines, the main commercial airline in Peru. TAPSA would fly to Pucallpa when the weather was bad, whereas Faucett wouldn't fly due to caution. An American pilot, a crew of four men, and eight Peruvian passengers went down with the TAPSA plane. We had to commit ourselves to God's keeping each time we flew over the rain forest.

On a Monday morning, I went over to visit the school to routinely help Gregorio. Irma decided to go fishing with a group of women.

*Cashibo-Cacataibo*

They crossed the river, walked on a small trail until it disappeared, and began cutting a trail. They came to a little stream, backwater left over from when the river was high. Irma stayed with Sara and Rita, but took her shoes off to preserve them. She left them where she removed them in order to pick them up on the way back, some distance from where they stopped to fish. The manner of fishing was interesting. They cut the leaves from a particular plant that grows around the clearing, mashed up the leaves with a rock and rolled them up in soft balls. At the river, they swished the leaf balls in the water until they dissolved. The poison that came out was whitish in color and clouded the water, stunning the fish. The fish flopped around as they absorbed the poison. One must hit them with a machete or stick and then pick them up with one's hands. The fish were like sunfish, about five to eight inches long. Many of them were smaller, but all were eaten. They were cleaned, then fried, head and all. The whole fish was eaten, including head and crispy fins.

As mentioned earlier, Irma had removed her shoes and left them back on the trail. After fishing, the women heard Rara's dogs barking and chasing something over in the forest. Rara called for Sara and Rita to come since the dogs were chasing an agouti (*mari* in Cashibo language). Sara and Rita took off through the jungle with Irma following barefoot. She had to pick her way carefully, but they hesitated for her. When they finally arrived to where Rara was, the animal had gone into a hole. They listened and kept digging along the length of the tunnel. After about fifteen minutes, Irma went to look and was amazed to see that they had an armadillo by the tail and were using a stick to keep it from going down any farther. They poked it with a machete, killed it, and pulled it out of the hole. They then decided to go and fish at another location. Irma kept stepping on thistles and thorns, repenting of the fact that she had left her shoes back on the trail. Experience is the best teacher. She helped them catch the fish and they really appreciated that. Also, when they arrived back home, the women said that because Irma was along, they had killed the armadillo, which was a delicious meal for them.

While Irma went fishing, I recorded more stories of the Cashibo culture told by Poloponte. These stories were about tribal migration and about their demigods, the Incas. In this culture, the Incas were not only the ancestors of the modern Quechuas, but also were light-skinned foreigners like Spaniards in the stories he told. The recorded narratives were needed to see how the grammar rules worked in context and would be used to translate the New Testament.

A little girl was brought to us with fungus on her foot. We treated it one day, but the parents decided it hadn't helped and they refused to bring her back for further treatment. Much later, they brought her again when the fungus was infected. She had a lump in her groin the size of a hen's egg as well as a little knot forming behind her knee. We gave her sulfa and penicillin and soon had a radio schedule with the medical doctor at Yarinacocha base. He recommended that we stop giving her sulfa, keep up the penicillin, and then give her duo-streptococcus injections along with the penicillin. This was to subdue the infection that had settled in the lymph node which we would then incise to let it drain. We dreaded doing the lancing, but it was necessary. As a result, the foot and lymph node healed nicely.

We made contact on the radio about having a service flight just before going upriver since the float plane can land at the wider downriver location. We were told that on that very day a plane was coming to bring visitors: Mr. and Mrs. Clarence Erickson from Des Moines, Iowa. He had produced the radio program "Heaven and Home Hour" for twenty years. Having heard of Irma's work in Peru, and since she was from Iowa, he decided to visit us in Peru. He made an audio tape-recorded interview with the two of us, using my reel-to-reel recorder. He planned to play it on six radio stations in Iowa and Wisconsin.

The plane brought a few things we needed, including an air mattress for Irma, so we decided we didn't need a service flight after all. However, Dean Sawdon, a fellow worker with Irma in the bookkeeping office at Yarinacocha base, talked with Irma on the radio saying that he and Priscilla, the woman she had been rooming with at the base, were planning to fly out to see us on Saturday. This was another surprise. Martha and Bob Weaver, workers on the base, also decided to come. They arrived at 9:30 Saturday morning and stayed until five o'clock in the afternoon.

The plane pulled up at the upper end of the water strip. We all walked up the hill to see Gregorio's school. After visiting, speaking Spanish there, we walked the fifteen minutes on the trail to our house. There we ate a scrumptious dinner they had brought and visited with one another. They took pictures, and we translated into English as we talked with the Cashibo. Martha and Priscilla went to the spring with us where Martha proceeded to join us in taking a cool bath on that hot tropical day. We walked back over the trail and the visitors left at five o'clock. We had plenty of food reminders that they had been there to visit us. They brought a dozen tomatoes, a dozen apples, meat loaf, pork roast, a dozen eggs, a kilo of onions, two carrots, four grapefruit, cheese, peanut butter fudge, mayonnaise, and margarine. Since we had no refrigerator, we had to eat it all soon. We had meat loaf sandwiches for dinner the next day, with tomatoes, pickles, and mustard. How delicious! Also, we had been given two pies and a large cake. We put the meat in a large pan in the cold spring water with large rocks on top. By the next day, it seemed like a dream that the visitors had come to the tribe to see us.

Soon after the visitors left, Tito Estrella, teacher Gregorio's younger brother, returned to the location where we were living. He was the husband of Rara in whose house we were living. Tito had left over a year ago and now had returned with his new Conibo (a branch of the Shipibo tribe) wife, baby boy, and his new wife's two other children. We were afraid Rara would get upset and start fighting with her co-wife. However, the house in which we lived was Tito's, but he and his new family just made themselves at home in Rara's new house until we left. Rara was quite a bit older than Tito and unable to bear children.

Soon after, we stopped a motorboat going by on a Monday, and asked the owner if he would take us upriver on Friday. The men on board agreed to do it for 250 soles Peruvian money, so we took them up on the offer. There are a number of motorboats on the river—at least six or eight—so we didn't have any trouble contracting for one.

On Wednesday, we were still eating from the food that our visitors had left on Saturday. The meat (beef and pork) was so good and lasted well in the coolness of the spring water. Otherwise, we would have been eating animals from the wild. We cooked the remaining meat in the pressure cooker to keep it from spoiling. The cake and pie lasted until Wednesday. We hated to see the gift food run out, for we had been eating like queens.

We packed all day Thursday and had many Indians come to say goodbye. Influenza was spreading due to the cold weather we had for a few days. One woman was sick with high fever when we left. We gave her medicine to take and hoped that she would recover. On Friday, May 29, we left our location on the lower Aguaytia, a place called Pacasmayo, at eight o'clock in the morning. Traveling by motorboat on a beautiful day with white clouds, we arrived at the bridge (Puente Aguaytia) at 11:30 in the morning. We went to the same hotel in which we stayed last time, but the owner was away in her garden. There was no other hotel close by and we didn't want to go too far from the river. The owner of the motorboat saw where we wanted to stay and told us to go ahead and take our baggage in. He proceeded to take the bed out of the room and put our belongings in there. We learned that he knew the people and stayed there himself at times, so we came with the right man. We unloaded all our baggage and left it in the care of two Cashibo boys who came upriver with us. We told them not to leave the room unattended; when one went out, the other was to stay in the room. Leaving at 1:45 p.m. we went a short way back downriver and arrived at the Reifsnyder port at 2:30 p.m. It was a delightful ride in the motorboat. When we arrived at the port, the two men in the motorboat carried our suitcases, and we set off hiking over the muddy, rather closed-in trail, arriving at their home a half-hour later. We were greeted warmly and given a guest bedroom in their home. We had a nice visit over the weekend, staying until Sunday afternoon about three o'clock. We said goodbye and thanked Mrs. Reifsnyder for her hospitality, then rode on mules with Mr. Reifsnyder leading us over the trail. We arrived at the road two hours later, then were driven by our host in his truck back to Puente Aguaytia. We arrived in time to attend the evangelical church service in Spanish.

When we arrived back at our room, our belongings were all intact and the two boys were in the room watching them. There were three canoe-loads of Indians in the town selling bananas, ostensibly from upriver, but Monday morning dawned and the upriver Cashibo-

Cacataibo had left without us. That day we shopped, visited the Chief of Police, and visited with the pastor of the church and his wife. We also visited with the *Sanitario* (a male nurse). He is the only one who practices medicine in the town. We had heard on Sunday evening when we returned to the bridge that a man in Shambuyacu named Maximo had been bitten by a snake the day after we left. The Cashibo boys from downriver were anxious to return home to take Maximo over to Reifsnyders' house for treatment. While we had been at our American friends' house, a man there was recuperating from a poisonous snakebite. The snake had bitten him just below his right eye. He was in poor condition for a few days since his head had swollen so dreadfully, but with the antidote the Reifsnyders gave him, he was almost totally recuperated in nine days. The cold water treatment to slow down the blood flow, new at that time, was really a marvelous discovery.

The male nurse showed us a letter from the government in Lima stating that, if he would send the names and ages of all the families in that area, they would supply free medicine for them. We supplied him with most of the names of the Native Americans, though we may have missed a few families. We were thrilled to hear about the government's offer and hoped the Cashibo-Cacataibo would take advantage of this when it became available.

Tuesday rolled around and still no Cashibo came for us. We saw a Peruvian man from a little way upriver whom we had met before. He said he would send one of his men upriver early Wednesday morning with our letter. Therefore, we wrote a letter urging them to come soon.

There was a nice stream running alongside Puente Aguaytia called the Black River because the water looked dark, possibly because it had some kind of mineral in it. It was probably spring-fed because it was always clean even when it rained. We were glad there was a nice place to bathe. Also, we were set up for cooking in our hotel room, thankful for the food we had with us. We actually had two rooms side by side. We put our air mattresses on the beds in the room and used our own sheets, so we were quite comfortable. But there were a few things to make us uncomfortable. Huge rats ran up and down the walls, and over the rafters. Once in a while they dropped down on our beds. Also, we only had a little potty—no bathroom. Finally, we located two Shipibo Indians who were willing to take us to the home of a Peruvian man named Gonzales about two or three hours upriver.

On Wednesday afternoon, June 3, a man named Antonio, his wife, and six children arrived from Pintayo with the purpose of taking us upriver. They had a large canoe, but we did not understand why he had brought his entire family of small children, five of them under seven years of age and the oldest boy being about twelve years old. We thought the river was low the last year, but it was high then compared to the present year. If we had known how low the river was in the areas of rapids, we wouldn't have had the courage to start out on that trip. Instead of two or three hours, the trip took five hours to Gonzales' house. We didn't get away from Puente Aguaytia until eleven o'clock that morning and arrived at Gonzales' house at four o'clock in the afternoon. We walked on the beaches as much as possible during the trip. Mr. Gonzales put us up for the night in a large wooden double bed in the same room in which he, his wife, daughter, and two sons were sleeping. Antonio and his family slept in a couple of small lean-tos.

We arose the next morning about 6:30, expecting that we would have a quick breakfast and be off on the rest of our trip. However, Gonzales was nowhere around. He had promised that there would be men there to take us the rest of the way, so we waited a while. Finally, the men came. Thanking the hostess for her hospitality, we left. Going was slow and rough. The farther we went upriver, each of the rapids was less shallow than the previous one. We felt that we had to help push the canoe through the rapids because the men would let the canoe sit in the rapids about ten minutes struggling to push the canoe through, yet not able to move an inch. With our added bit of help, we were able to inch through the rapids, pushing with all our might. Some places the rushing river water was up to our hips; other places it was only half way up our legs. At times, we had to pull rocks out from under the canoe to push it through.

We would proceed a short distance and meet a Peruvian *mestizo* family, then another. We asked if someone would please help us, but it was always the same story—they were on their way downriver with bananas and plantain to sell at the bridge. Anyway, why should they help us? They didn't know us. Irma said she felt very bad taking such a heavy load of belongings upriver, making the Cashibo family push the weight through the many rapids. We wondered what they were thinking, and whether our help would ever repay what it cost them to get us there. If only the river were long and deep enough between rapids for a pontoon plane to land!

At three o'clock in the afternoon, we arrived at the place where Gonzales' brother, Lucho, lived. As we arrived at Lucho's place, it began to rain heavily, so we were invited to stay all night at his house. He was very cordial and said that he and his brother would take us the rest of the way the next day. This was music to our ears. We were so exhausted and stressed by such a hard trip that we didn't eat very much of the good Peruvian supper of boiled chicken and bananas. We were bedded down in their double bed while the parents with their family slept on the floor. What hospitality! Actually, they had been sleeping on the floor for some months because their family had grown too large for the bed. To keep warm, they all slept together on the floor under their mosquito net.

The next day dawned gray, cloudy, and drizzly. We hoped within our hearts that Lucho would not change his mind since we were anxious to arrive at our destination. We ate a hearty breakfast of boiled plantain with boiled eggs, thanked our host and hostess, and left at 8:30 in the morning. We rode in the canoe about the first ten minutes, then decided to get out and walk. We hadn't intended to walk the rest of the way, but it was so much easier for them not to bother with us getting in and out of the canoe. We kept finding trails where the jungle was next to the river going from one beach to the next. Antonio's wife walked with us, carrying her two-month-old baby in her arms and had two little boys tagging along beside her as naked as the day they were born. Little boys were not required to wear clothes until they reached puberty, about eleven years old. It began to rain and each member of Antonio's family carried a banana leaf over his or her head as a makeshift umbrella. We had our ponchos to keep us warm and dry. The mother had banana leaves draped all over the baby, who nursed while awake, then dropped off to sleep for a while.

Some of the trails we came across were nearly grown over, causing us to bend over or even crawl in some places because we were so tall. We were fearful of encountering snakes, but, thankfully, we didn't see any. The twelve-year-old boy of the Cashibo family was our guide, so we had no fear of losing our way. We were way ahead of the canoe. When we would walk out on a beach, we couldn't see the canoe at all. We hoped they weren't wondering where we were, but it was too cold and rainy to wait and tell them where we were. We came to the old location of Pintayo and decided to cross the river at this point. Holding each other's hands, we all waded across. It was only hip high in the deepest place, which wasn't bad. Just as we arrived on the other side of the river, we looked back across the river and saw Juan Chavez's bull looking at us. Juan was a leader for this upriver group. We hurried down the trail and arrived at 11:30 a.m., just three hours after we started. The canoe with all our belongings arrived an hour later giving us time to clean up the thatch-roofed hut in which we were to stay. It was located on a sandy clearing a few feet higher than the river and about thirty feet from the bank.

Our belongings we had left there were just as we had left them, although the shelf holding them was ready to collapse. Martin Cardenes, one of the Cashibo men, was making our single size beds. The bed legs were planted in the ground since we had a dirt floor. Last year we had brought our own aluminum frame folding beds but left them at Yarinacocha base this year. Martin rebuilt the broken shelf, then made another shelf for us. We started settling into our old hut.

For two days we arranged our belongings. On Monday we had enough sun to dry out most of the important goods. On Tuesday we were ready to get to work. Martin very much wanted to be a bilingual school teacher, though we were not sure that he was able. He had such an earnest desire to teach that we decided to give him a trial teaching time for three months. He would not be paid, but he was eager to do it even without pay. That time of testing and observing would be proof of whether to take him to the base for further training. Unfortunately, he did not pass the test, and we had to look for another young man to be a teacher.

We gave out one shotgun shell to each of three men who had guns. We asked them to give us a thigh and leg of the animals killed as payment for each shell. What a landslide it started! In five days we received three legs of wild animals, a large piece of deer meat, and two fish. One of the animals was killed with a bow and arrow, but otherwise all the shells were used. We had so much meat we didn't know what to do with all of it. We pressure cooked and ate what we could, and the rest we shared with our neighbors. It is cheaper than the meat we buy in cans and much tastier.

A family of rats was living in our palm-thatched roof. The children came over to visit every night since we had the bright light of a gasoline pressure lantern. One night the boys came with little bows and arrows and killed two large rats, the mother and father rats. The next night we heard the baby rats squeaking, so the little boys shook them out of the roof and killed them. As you can imagine, we had our excitement at times.

Tuberculosis was rampant there. The people lived in thatch-roofed huts with no walls, allowing the cool, damp air to blow through the house, especially in rainy season. If the homes had cane pole walls, that was still not much protection. There was a young man about thirty years of age who had a hopeless case of terminal tuberculosis. He was a handsome fellow who took tuberculosis medicine for it for a year, medicine procured from Dr. Swanson at Yarinacocha base. He was to continue getting injections from Mr. Reifsnyder downriver, but began to feel better and neither took the medicine nor went for the injections. We had to tell him that his case was hopeless, though we spoke with great regret. We did not know the language well enough to tell him the gospel, a great need since he had only a few weeks to live. Later on, Dr. Douglas Swanson held three clinics at Lower Aguaytia, Upper Aguaytia, and Sinchi Roca on the San Alejandro River. As a result, we found that sixty percent of the Cashibo-Cacataibo had tuberculosis. With his help, we were able to pinpoint just which persons needed treatment.

I worked with Heriberto Pacarua, a thirty-nine-year-old shaman, to record a text about rain forest medicine from that upriver area on the Aguaytia. He told of various medicinal plants used to cure common ailments of the people. Heriberto treated both Cashibo and *mestizo* patients. He told various stories about when animals were like humans and could talk. He also told about the process of cremation and practice of endocannibalism. The people used to cremate the body of their loved one, scrape the ashes out and put them in a drink. They believed that those who drank the mixture would receive qualities and characteristics of the dead person. This was no longer practiced on the Aguaytia River.

The upriver people talked about clearing a landing strip for the Helio Courier plane, the airplane that can land and take off on short airstrips. We had heavy rains for three weeks. Especially on a Wednesday and Thursday, June 24 and 25, the yearly *San Juan* cold, rainy weather took place. It caused the river to rise to flood stage. We had the idea of having a pontoon plane come. Our gasoline for the Briggs and Stratton generator was almost gone since we left our seven gallon container of gas at Puente Aguaytia to make our load not so heavy coming upriver. On Thursday, we called the base about one o'clock, and a plane started out on the trip; however, it ran into a storm on the way and had to return to Yarinacocha. We figured that was the end of the plane trip since the river would only stay up about five hours at the most. We did not call the base by radio, but, surprisingly, about eleven o'clock on Friday morning, we heard a plane overhead. The Indians said it was going to land, but Irma laughed and said it couldn't land since the river was too low. I was on the radio talking to the base as the pilot was circling and circling. We didn't have direct contact with the pilot so the base had to be the intermediary. The pilot suggested that we have several men wade across the river so he could see how deep it was and where. The men began wading and the water reached up to their armpits. At one end of the strip a man had to swim, but the strip of deep water did not look long enough. Pilot George kept circling, then began to land and he made it fine. However, he said he wouldn't care to try it again. We were so glad to get the gasoline and other items we had ordered, such as salt, alcohol for lighting our Primus pressure burner for cooking, and other items. Also, a number of people at Yarinacocha base sent candy, cookies, cheese, fresh tomatoes, and potatoes. We feasted for several days.

We didn't hand out more than one shell to a hunter every few days since handing out so many previously had brought in a flood of meat. We had tender and delicious deer steaks, venison burgers, wild hog meat, and, occasionally, a fish or two. We only opened two cans of meat in three weeks.

On Sunday, June 21, Juan Chavez, the former teacher and chief of this area, came down with everyone from upriver. Altogether, we had eighteen men besides women and children there. We gave them popcorn as a treat, and they had a palaver. They decided to clear an area for an airstrip in a high flat area. They also talked about the land for which they were soliciting, how much they were going to own, and how very little of it they were actually occupying. They had no idea how to go about getting the land papers of ownership at that time.

On the way home from visiting with us, one of the little boys, a son of the shaman Chaparina, was bitten by a snake. His father treated him and the boy recovered. His father was about thirty-two years old, nice looking, and wore neat Western clothing. The older men used medicinal plants from the forest, but the shamans also drank *ayahuasca* drug, a cooked plant from the forest, to see colorful visions along with chanting, blowing, and sucking on the patient's skin to remove evil spirits.

Irma began a school for the children since Martin did not work out as a teacher. She had a total of twelve children enrolled and found that these children, who lacked experience with paper, pencils, words or numbers, were difficult to teach. They had a hard time realizing the value of numbers. Irma felt like the Pied Piper since all the children followed her along the fifteen-minute walk to the school hut. The children were singing, jumping, talking, and laughing, full of life and mischief. She enjoyed the children tremendously. Although it was a real test of patience to teach them, their smiles and responses were worth every minute of it. She strove to show love and understanding to them in every way.

*Eight Years in the Amazon Headwaters*

Bolivar and child bride

One day a man named Bolivar, about sixty years old, came to see us and with him was a little girl about eight years old. She was a member of Antonio's family who brought our canoe-load of equipment upriver. We thought she had no connections, but upon asking, we discovered that she was the elderly man's wife. He said he was raising her for his wife. Antonio, her father, had too many mouths to feed, and an older man could pay a better bride price than a young man could. He made a deal with Bolivar, giving his daughter to him in exchange for a shotgun. Because of a shortage of women, there were many men who needed wives. Bolivar was one of the previous chiefs of the tribe, so Antonio gained prestige by giving his daughter to him. The fathers preferred having boy babies to help them work and, as a result, often practiced infanticide of girl babies. This caused a shortage of women for brides. A few years later, Bolivar's young wife became a beautiful teen-ager. Most of the young wives raised from childhood despised their elderly husbands. Martin's wife was an example of this.

Martin worked for his father-in-law Isacamo for many years while his child bride was growing up. Martin was an orphan and could not pay for his wife, therefore, he worked for his father-in-law. When we first arrived she was about nine or ten years old. Later, when she went through puberty, she became pregnant and had a cute baby girl. Martin was ecstatic. But behind the scenes, Martin's wife despised him and became infatuated with a teen-age boy. One day they "eloped," taking Martin's child with them. They went to live downriver, choosing to live and work among the Spanish-speaking *mestizos*, abandoning their Cashibo ties. Martin was devastated and heart-broken. Now all the years he worked to gain his child bride were for nothing.

Irma and I finished our stay with the upriver people and returned to Yarinacocha base. Shortly thereafter, Dean Sawdon proposed to Irma and she happily accepted, so I lost my tribal partner. They were married in a civil ceremony in Pucallpa on September 23, 1959, then on September 29 had a religious ceremony at Yarinacocha. So for a while she continued working at the base finance office with Dean. They had a daughter named Kari born February 6, 1961, in the United States while they were home on furlough. After the Sawdons returned to the base and the Cashibo-Cacataibo would come to Yarinacocha, they enjoyed visiting Irma and seeing her young child. Irma was happy to be able to speak their language when visiting with them.

## *CHAPTER 20: THE YEAR 1960*

In 1960, my fifth year in the Peruvian rain forest, my new partner was a SIL/WBT member named Harriet Fields from Indiana. She was with me temporarily for two years, then later entered another Pano language family tribe. She brought with her to the Aguaytia and San Alejandro Rivers a light-weight, battery-driven, audio cassette tape recorder which was much easier to carry than my heavy, electric reel-to-reel recorder and motor. As a result, we were able to make better recordings without the background noise of the Briggs and Stratton generator.

Puerto Azul community along the airstrip

Our first trip was to the Aguaytia River upriver location where a short airstrip had been cleared and prepared for landing and takeoff. It was approved by the JAARS pilots for the Helio Courier plane. There were two rows of huts, one on each side of the airstrip. The leaders of the area named the community *Puerto Azul*,"Blue Port." We were assigned a hut on the side toward the Aguaytia River. Each night of dry season when the river was low, we could hear the water rushing over the rocks of the rapids. Our thatched-roof hut had cane pole walls with a nice raised porch where the children loved to come to look at scrapbook pictures and to color with crayons in coloring books. We also kept a photo album with pictures of Cashibo-Cacataibo people that was their favorite book to peruse.

My main activity was to record histories and narratives in the Cashibo language for study of paragraph structure, how sentences were put together, and how reference was made to different persons in the stories. I turned the medical work over to Harriet who was learning the language quickly. She was well-liked, joking with the teen-age young men. They would sit on a log along one side of the airstrip conversing with Harriet and laugh every few minutes.

I would tell a Bible story on Sundays, using a set of flannel graph figures on a cloth board for illustration. Generally, those who came were children and teen-agers. When invited, the women would say, "I can't come because I don't have any nice dresses." We would say, "Oh, come just as you are. Your dress is fine." But they never came. So we had to talk with them individually.

After hearing that Jesus had died to pay for his sins, one Cashibo-Cacataibo young man named Lizardo Nyana asked Jesus to come into his life. He studied a year or two at the Swiss Indian Mission Bible School. Later, he made a trip with us to the San Alejandro River to preach to the Cacataibo branch of the tribe. Unfortunately, later in life he became a bilingual school teacher and encountered many problems in his life.

One evening at *Puerto Azul* after the people had retired into their huts to sleep, we heard a loud roar coming from the forest near the settlement. It was a jaguar. None of the houses had doors or any way to keep the animal out. Fear spread through the huts. Again and again the wild, big cat roared. Men had rifles and bows and arrows ready in case the jaguar would come out into the open space of the airstrip. But the roars finally came from farther away and then disappeared. Our hearts stopped pounding and we all went to sleep, except for a few men who kept guard in case the wild animal would come back again.

One man told a story about camping at night while on a hunting trip. They were sleeping around a fire. All of a sudden a man cried out. A jaguar had sneaked quietly into the camp, bitten off a large piece of the man's buttock, and run away. The men were thoroughly frightened and sat up the rest of the night. In the wee hours of the morning, they broke camp and headed for home with their guns ready in case they would see the jaguar again. Long afterward, they told this story and everyone laughed about the man who lost a piece of his buttock to the jaguar.

I recorded histories from the elderly man named Isacamo. He told how the tribe used to be more numerous and had large houses having thatched roofs which extended clear down to the ground. He told that by warring with each other and by illnesses from the white men, there were now only a few people left in the tribe. Sadly, he told me that he felt like a tree standing alone after all the rest of the forest had been cut down around it.

Harriet and I finally left *Puerto Azul* in the upper Aguaytia River area. We went downriver to Puente Aguaytia town, but on the way our canoe began leaking. We had a couple of tin cans we used to bail out the water, but the water gained on us and we were about to be swamped. We came to a canoe port at that time, where there was a canoe available for us to borrow. We transferred our belongings to the dry canoe just in time to keep from soaking everything in that canoe. Fortunately, we had most of our belongings in another canoe, which didn't leak.

At Puente Aguaytia town, where the roadway crossed the river, we caught a ride on a truck and rode over the twisting, winding gravel road to the San Alejandro River, a much smaller river than the Aguaytia. Along the way, we saw small, beautiful, pink orchids growing wild on the hillsides. Arriving at the town of San Alejandro, we unloaded our belongings from the truck. Some Spanish-speaking *mestizos* from this small community offered to take us up to Sinchi Roca near the mouth of the Chanintia River, a small stream that emptied into the San Alejandro River. We loaded our belongings into their boat, the only time we ever had a small roof covering us as we traveled. It was nice to have protection from the tropical sun. We arrived at Sinchi Roca and said, "*Adios*" (Goodbye) to our Peruvian friends. Teacher Alfonso Perez Flores met us, and we spent a few days there visiting with the Cacataibo people. We recorded the life history of Alfonso. He also told a humorous story of a man who stole an accordion from the white people in Pucallpa. When he pulled and pushed, it made noise, so he thought it must be an Inca demigod. But when all the people came down with diarrhea (the amoeba intestinal parasite which he had contracted from the whites), he thought the accordion must be an evil spirit. The people became angry and shot it with their bows and arrows, then threw it in the river after salvaging some parts to use for decorations.

The tribal men chanted in a form called *no bana* (naw vahnah, "enemies' words"). This style of singing in a single high note being repeated in cadence could be carried out in a quiet type or a loud, forceful type. It was often used to praise the moon goddess, but was also used to tell stories about one's ancestors and early life. We recorded several of these chants in Sinchi Roca while we were living in a hut with the teacher and his family.

In September, we set out in canoes headed for the settlement called Criminal (the same in English and Spanish). It was about a two- or three-day trip upriver. We camped out on the sandy beaches in this low-water dry season. There were only a few lean-tos with leaf roofs to keep the dew off at night at one beach. One other night there were no lean-tos, so we laid out a piece of plastic on which to lie and also had a large piece of plastic to cover both us and the Cacataibo people. During the night, a tropical storm broke, and we tried to keep the plastic over all of us during the downpour which lasted for about an hour. Those on the outside edges were getting wet, but as a whole we escaped getting soaked. Lizardo Nyana from *Puerto Azul* accompanied us on this trip to Criminal village. The group was so-named because a posse of twelve Peruvian white men had gone upriver to the tribal settlement years before to try to "civilize" the upriver Cacataibo people, meaning to teach them and acculturate them to white men's ways. Instead, all twelve of the men were killed by the tribal men. We wondered how the people at Criminal would receive us.

After the long trip, we arrived upriver at Criminal. We two North American women were quartered in a small hut with four, cane-pole walls all the way around the sleeping room and one opening which served as a doorway. Every night a man kept watch just outside the doorway, hopefully to protect us. During the day, we were watched closely by a woman who followed us even when we wanted to relieve ourselves away from the other people. We began to have the feeling that we were in a dangerous place, but we knew that God would take care of us. Lizardo found opportunity to preach to them, to tell them about Jesus and how He died to pay for the sins of all people.

One man there was called *Caman No* meaning "Land Enemy." He was the last remaining man of his group—all the rest of his tribe had been killed. From him we recorded a loud war cry that he demonstrated while he rocked back and forth on his heels, holding up a crossed bow and arrow.

We asked if we could go into the river to bathe, but the people said it would be better not to since there were electric eels there. We decided to wash from a pan of water in our room.

The people were processing manioc roots, an interesting event. They poured water into a canoe full of peeled manioc. The manioc was soaked for a few days to soften it, then the canoe was drained. The women took the inner root strings out of the softened manioc and put it through a round, basket-weave sieve to form small pieces similar to our Grape-Nuts cereal. The soft pieces were roasted in a pan over a hot fire to dry them out. This cereal-like manioc was later mixed with water to soften it for eating, a food easy to carry on a hunting trip.

Two women and two children had bodies that were covered with sores. We thought that it was due to not having soap with which to wash off bacteria, so we gave them some soap. In just a few days, the sores were clearing up.

We recorded some women's chants aside from the men's chants and stories, and the time to leave soon came. We were relieved to be departing from the strain of being so closely watched. We packed up and floated downriver to Sinchi Roca. Floating downriver with the strong current shortened our trip to one day instead of the three days it took to come upriver.

One of the men at Sinchi Roca killed a doe and brought back its fawn to raise as a pet. Another man shot an armadillo and brought its young one to us. We put it in a basket and tied it shut, but it escaped into the wild during the night.

Our stay on the San Alejandro River finally ended. We packed our duffel bags, loaded our belongings into a canoe, and were paddled downriver to the village of San Alejandro where the road from Lima to Pucallpa crossed the river. There had been another tropical storm which made the swift river rise. Our Spanish-speaking, Peruvian friends were upset because a man had tried to swim across the swollen river a few days before and never made it across. He was submerged and drowned. His body was carried downriver and lost. The day that we arrived, the river was lower, and his body had been found. The family was grieving but also upset because they didn't have money to pay for a casket. The law was that the body had to be buried right away. A casket was being made and people in the small village pooled their money to help the distraught widow. We donated some Peruvian money to the fund.

While traveling on the San Alejandro River, we saw several locations where black oil was floating along the banks. It had the colors of the rainbow. Later, we reported this to an oil company. Some months later, they moved into the area, even building United States style frame houses in which the workers would live. They drilled upriver from the village. Their presence made drastic changes to San Alejandro village, such as widening the road through the town. Even so, they did not find enough oil to set up production and, as a result, the North Americans soon moved away.

Harriet and I returned to Yarinacocha base by road. She left working with the Cashibo to begin trying to reach the Mayoruna, another Pano language people. That tribe had stolen Peruvian women from the town of Requena north on the Ucayali River. I had the opportunity to fly to a meeting in the city of Iquitos with Norma Faust and James Loriot (formerly Lauriault) of SIL. James had grown up at Yarinacocha Lake and knew the Shipibo language well. At a meeting there, we each read Spanish linguistic papers we had written about the Indian languages with which we had worked. Also, we had been given the job of looking for a Peruvian white woman who had been captured by the Mayorunas but had later escaped from them. James Loriot was the head of our project to find this woman. He had several leads, and we finally contacted

*Eight Years in the Amazon Headwaters*

someone who knew where the woman lived. We were thrilled to find her and to hear her story.

She had been captured by the tribesmen and taken to their settlement where she was given as wife to one of their leaders. She did not know their language, but was forced to learn it quickly by being burned with firebrands when she didn't understand and obey. She showed us the many scars she had over her body from being burned by hot coals. Her clothes wore out and she had to go naked like the native women. She had a daughter by her Indian husband. The daughter grew up to teen-age, married one of the tribesmen, and even presented her mother with a grandbaby. But the captured white woman always looked for a way to escape. Finally, she found her chance. While working alone in the garden near a river, she ran to the river and swam downriver as fast as she could. She eventually arrived at a Peruvian soldiers' outpost. They gave her one of their uniforms to cover her naked body, then took her out to the city of Requena and on to the large city of Iquitos where she could feel safe.

It was to this tribe that Harriet Fields, with her new partner Hattie Kneeland, committed themselves to learn the Mayoruna language and to translate the New Testament for them. The opportunity finally came in 1969 after months of calling to the people in phrases and sentences of their language from a distance. Thankfully, no one was hurt and they eventually entered the Mayoruna tribe. Within a year, they had a large house with a palm-thatched roof built for them, and they were peacefully learning the language of the people now called the Matses.

## CHAPTER 21: FURLOUGH

In January of 1961, I returned to the United States for a furlough after five years in Peru. I flew by way of Mexico where my brother, Kent Wistrand, and his wife, Mary Lou, under the auspices of WBT and SIL were learning the Xayacatlan Mixtec language, a very difficult tonal language. Eventually, after 25 years, they had learned it well and translated the New Testament into that language. They met me in Mexico City and gave me a tour of the Latin American tower, the Shrine of Guadalupe, and other interesting sites. Then I flew on to Houston, Texas, for a grand reunion with my family. In the spring semester of 1961, I enrolled to study some courses at the University of Houston while living at home with my parents.

In the summer of 1961, I enrolled with SIL International in the University of Oklahoma at Norman for the third year linguistic workshop. My goal was to study Cashibo-Cacataibo narrative structure in order to work on translation of narrative materials, such as the stories of the life of Jesus in the Gospels of the New Testament. Internationally known SIL linguist Dr. Kenneth Pike was teaching the class of SIL workers who had one or more five-year terms on the field. My dorm roommate was Jean Shand who had been my roommate in our first summer of 1954. Jean had just completed her five-year term in the Philippine Islands. Dr. Pike's lectures were on his tagmemic approach to paragraph and episode structure. Dr. Viola Waterhouse worked with me on an article describing Cashibo-Cacataibo sentence and paragraph structure. That summer, along with the two previous summers I had studied at the University of Oklahoma SIL, earned me twenty-five hours of university credit in linguistics.

In the fall semester, I enrolled at the University of Texas at Austin, with a major in linguistics and minor in anthropology. I also took two five-hour courses in classical Greek to help in translation. I used my experiences in Peru to write up papers in anthropology and linguistics. In the cultural anthropology class, the professor was an eighty-year-old man who had been born in Spain but who had worked against the government such that he had to flee to Mexico.

Then he took part in an uprising against the government in Mexico's civil war in 1910. Therefore, he once again had to flee, this time to the United States. In his course plans, he included a unit on the Jivaro Indians. When I told him that I had worked with the Jivaroan Aguarunas in Peru, he asked me to take a class period to show my slides of Aguaruna life. I gladly consented and had a good time answering questions from the students after showing the slides. Unfortunately, the summer after my course with him, the professor died in Mexico on an anthropological study trip.

During my time in the USA, I also spoke in many churches and showed my slides while telling of my experiences. This was partly to raise more support since my pledged support was only around $125.00 per month, not much income even at that time. Monetary support was given by my home church and various individuals among family and friends.

The time came for me to again pack my two fifty-five gallon barrels of equipment and clothing to take to Peru. My size of women's sneakers was not available in Peru at that time, so I packed all of them in the barrels for the next term. Ladies at the church made some nice cotton print dresses for me to wear, and these were also packed in the barrels. They were simple dresses made of strong cloth that would last being beaten on the rocks along the rivers. Once again I said goodbye to all my family and friends and flew from Houston to Miami, then on the long trip to Lima, Peru.

# CHAPTER 22: BEGINNING MY SECOND TERM

Even though it was summer season when I left home for Peru, it was mid-winter in Lima when I arrived that June. Friends from the WBT/SIL center in Lima met me at the airport and took me to a room at Cudney House, the SIL center in Lima. It was named for Mrs. Cudney, the housemother, a wonderful woman. There I settled for the night, weary from the trip. In the morning I woke to the screeches of someone's pet parrot and to a cold room, for there was no heat in most homes in Lima. Even so, I was thankful to be back in Peru. After a few days in Lima to check in at the American Embassy and make reservations to fly out to Pucallpa, I flew over the majestic, snow-covered Andes Mountains, across the foothills of the Andes including the Aguaytia and San Alejandro Rivers, then over the flat rain forest to Pucallpa on the Ucayali River. It was hot and humid as I stepped out of the plane and was met by friends from nearby Yarinacocha base. We traveled the bumpy, unpaved road out to the base, which was a beehive of activity.

One major project at the base was to have a house built with Carol Whisler. We were both fairly tall and thin, both had blonde hair and wore glasses, and both had similar last names, so some people confused us with one another. We both also had brothers in WBT/SIL in other countries. Carol worked for a while with the Campa tribe, using her artistic talents to illustrate Campa primers for teaching reading. Then she worked at the base on special assignments. When the house was built, we were thankful for our screened-in home with living room, kitchen, small dining room, two bedrooms, bathroom, office, and study room for working with the Indians. In the hallway between our bedrooms, we had a closed-in shelf where we kept a light bulb burning to keep the air dry for cameras and film since they would so easily mold or mildew in the tropical air. We slept under a blanket or quilt in the dry season since the air cooled down at night, though the days were hotter than in the wet season.

We had one fifteen-year-old *mestiza* maid who came from off the base to clean the floors, take the dirty clothes to the centralized washing machine, hang up the clothes to dry in the sun, and iron. She did a pretty good job, but did not seem to like waxing the floors. I got down on my hands and knees and helped her rub the wax on the floor, then buffered it to a nice shine. "See how pretty it is," I said in Spanish. So the next time she waxed the floor by herself while I was away, as I entered the house she greeted me with the happy expression, "See how pretty it is!" pointing to the newly waxed floor. She had learned how to do it. But later on, after she had cleaned my room by herself, I found my comb black, probably from smoke of cooking fires back home, and with tell-tale black hairs. Also, my clothes gave evidence of having been tried on. After that I cleaned my own room.

Aside from working with the Cashibo-Cacataibo, I was on the literacy committee as advisor to tribe workers who were putting together primers which were beginning readers and writing books for their respective tribal languages. They were supposed to introduce a limited number of alphabet letters with sufficient repetition and review of new words to make learning easy. This took some of my time at the base and gave me experience in working with different languages.

Most of the SIL/WBT single folks who lived in their own houses made their own breakfasts but went to the central dining room for lunch and dinner. This gave more time for working on the tribal languages. Since linguistic work is intensive sit-down work and very tiring, after dinner we usually played volleyball to relax and get some exercise.

Bilingual school training of tribal teachers took place at the base January through March. Those teachers who had access came by road or river; the rest from farther away came by plane. They studied in classes taught in Spanish by professors from Lima and Pucallpa. But since their Spanish proficiency was usually very limited, they needed help on their classwork from the translators in the evenings. Thus, in those months, the base was crowded and full of activity. Linguists, supporting base workers, and Spanish-speaking professors were all busy training Indian teachers (many with their families) to move ahead in their education. At that time, tribal teachers were studying on primary (elementary) level, working to keep ahead of their students. With time they moved up to secondary school, and, eventually, some achieved college level.

# CHAPTER 23: WORKING WITH PEOPLE FROM ANOTHER MISSION

While Olive Shell was still in the United States and I was without a partner, I decided to visit the Cacataibo people on the San Alejandro River. A married couple from another mission had built a western-style, frame house and cleared a landing strip right next to their house. Bill and Alice (not their real names) spoke only Spanish to the Indians since they considered the Cacataibo a pagan language. They felt that the people needed to forget their own language and culture to learn Spanish and Western ways. They had a little store where they sold useful things like fish hooks, fish line, needles, and thread to the people. They also had Bible lessons which Bill told in Spanish but which his Cacataibo interpreter could not understand very well. Therefore, the interpreter just made general comments on what was being said in Spanish, interspersed with "I don't understand what he is saying." Also, Bill was gathering the older children and adolescents, speaking to them only in Spanish, and holding parties and meetings just for them. The parents complained to me in Cacataibo that their children were not obeying them and were doing things which the Cacataibo considered immoral. I tried to be a peacemaker and mediator between the two sides.

Tournavista was a settlement established by the LeTourneau family company while they used their huge earth-moving machines to build a road from Tournavista to the main road from Lima to Pucallpa. Not far from Tournavista, there were Peruvian workers trying to harvest saleable timber of the forest to sell for making lumber. But these men were hindered in their work by some Indians who opposed them. The Indians would dig deep pits in the trails with razor-sharp spears planted upright in them and cover the holes carefully so that they could not be seen. The timber workers were falling into these traps and badly injuring their legs and bodies.

When Bill heard of this, he took three Shipibo Indian men and hunted out the ones building the traps. The hunted ones were four Native Americans: a young man, elderly man, a young woman and elderly woman. These Indians had been sleeping in the daytime and working in their gardens at night to escape being killed or caught by the white men. Because of this, their skin was very light colored. Bill and his men located the four and fought with them for two hours before overcoming and subduing them. They were brought to the San Alejandro River Cacataibo community while I was there and placed in a hut under guard. I went in to talk with them in Cashibo-Cacataibo language since they spoke a related Pano language. They had been given a mosquito net that the older woman put on as a skirt bunched around her waist and thighs. The younger woman had put a pair of panties on her head, not knowing what they were to be used for. The young man had on a woman's dress slantwise, not knowing what the armholes were for. They had the custom of going naked and did not understand how to wear Western clothing.

A large fish about a foot long was brought to the captives, along with a metal pot to cook it in. The four had lived up in the headwaters where only very small fish were found. The young man pushed one side of the whole fish down and the other side stuck out of the pot. This took place several times. The people did not know how to cut up the large fish into smaller pieces and cook it in a pot. The Cacataibo showed them how to cut up the fish and cooked it for them. Then the strangers enjoyed eating the pieces of large fish.

When I entered and sat down to talk with them, the young man saw the buttons down the front of my dress and quickly took hold of one with one hand and moved his right hand holding a sharpened shell as a knife ready to cut the button off. I remonstrated in Cashibo-Cacataibo language, telling him the white lady would give him some other buttons. I recorded some of their language and noticed some similarities with Cashibo-Cacataibo language.

Later, an airplane came and landed on the strip by Bill and Alice's house. Everyone in the Cacataibo community ran to see the plane and the pilot. Even those guarding the four captives left their jobs and ran to see the plane. I wondered what the four captives were doing, so I hurried to their little hut. Just as I approached, three of the captives were leaving the hut and running into the forest to their freedom. The older man had decided to stay with the Cacataibo and sat quietly in the hut. I ran to tell the people of the flight of the three captives. The Cacataibo men went looking for them but never found them. The one captive who remained thought he was treated well and eventually was acculturated to the life of the Cacataibo.

# *CHAPTER 24: TRIP TO SUNGARO*

A group of the Cashibo-Cacataibo lived in the headwaters of the Sungaroyacu River, Sungaro for short. This river flowed into the Pachitea River which flowed into the Ucayali River. I didn't have a regular partner at that time, but when I asked Alice, with whom I had stayed on the San Alejandro River, she graciously accepted to leave her husband for a while to be my partner. We packed our belongings and set the flight date. When the day came, our equipment was loaded into the plane, we boarded, and the plane took off. The flight took us south up the Ucayali River, then up the Pachitea River to the town of Puerto Inca at the mouth of the Sungaro River. There we deplaned and contracted with some Peruvians to take us west, upriver in a motorboat to distant Santa Marta, the community of Cashibo-Cacataibo. We loaded our equipment into the boat, then moved quickly along the river against the current due to the powerful motor. Even so, it was an all-day trip to reach the Indians in the headwaters. We arrived at sundown.

The Indians at Puerto Azul on the Upper Aguaytia River always said, "Those people over at Santa Marta are bad—they kill people!" But then after we arrived at Santa Marta the Indians there said, "Oh, those people at the Upper Aguaytia River are bad. They kill people." So the feeling was mutual. We hoped that someday they would have peace and love for one another.

Some years before we arrived at Santa Marta, a Peruvian teacher from Puerto Inca went up the Sungaro River to teach the Indians in Spanish, but after only a few years of teaching, he died. Later, a Peruvian Catholic priest went up to Santa Marta to be a missionary and teach school. After a few years, he also died. Life was difficult at that location distantly upriver from Western civilization. Even for the Cashibo-Cacataibo, life was difficult, but having the local Native Americans as bilingual school teachers helped since they were born there and used to life in the headwaters.

We arrived and made new friends at Santa Marta. We were shown to the hut assigned to us, unpacked our belongings, and set up for the night. It was dark soon and we were tired from the all-day trip. The next day one of the first things we noticed was the presence of biting gnats—as bad or worse than in the Candoshi tribe. I would say worse. Fortunately, we had brought plenty of insect repellant which was used profusely. The Cashibo-Cacataibo called it *sioca* meaning "place of many gnats." These gnats swarmed around one's head, arms, and legs.

The bilingual school teacher accepted us graciously. Alice could not speak or understand the Cashibo-Cacataibo language, but she could speak Spanish with the bilingual teacher. I spent a lot of time helping the bilingual teacher as in previous visits to bilingual schools. Alice took care of most of the cooking and dishwashing since I was busy talking with the Indians in their language. Up until this time, none of the young men spoke or understood enough Spanish to go to the Swiss Indian Mission (SIM) Bible School. The local bilingual school was good preparation for some of the students to later go to Pucallpa to the SIM school. The Bible courses there were taught in Spanish and greatly helped the Native Americans from various tribes to speak and understand better Spanish along with their study of the Bible. Later, Gregorio Estrella Odicio and his wife Delfina were assigned to teach and live at Santa Marta. Delfina had been born and raised at Santa Marta, but married at a young age and went to live on the lower Aguaytia. She was highly acculturated to life on the Aguaytia River away from the gnats and nearer to Puente Aguaytia and, at her return to Santa Marta after so many years, she did not like the more primitive way of life at Sungaro. They only stayed there a few years, and returned to the Aguaytia River location where Gregorio once again taught at the bilingual school.

I had been collecting and pressing some tree leaves and smaller plants on the Aguaytia River and also collected some plants at Santa Marta. I asked for information about the use of the plants. There was a plant called *ucha ro,* "sin medicine," growing in that area which was used in olden days for testing by a shaman to see if a person was guilty of adultery or other wrongdoing. The leaf would be put on top of some water in a container. The leaf would act in one of two ways: either lay still, or move back and forth in quick movements. If it laid still, the person was innocent; if it moved quickly, the person was guilty. Usually, this test was used for a woman suspected of cheating on her husband. Someone later told me that the key to the leaf's action was the temperature of the water, whether it was warm or cold. Thus, the shaman could put the leaf in warm or cold water, depending on whether he considered the person guilty or innocent. If the woman was found guilty she was killed, usually shot by her husband with a bow and arrow. Some of the older men had killed one or more wives for this reason.

Later, after leaving Peru, I took my list of plants with their descriptions and uses to combine with a list collected by Dr. Olive Shell. Together they formed a small book named *Cashibo Flora*. There were medicinal plants for pain in all parts of the body: ear, teeth, throat, heart, stomach, and so on. There were contraceptive plants: one to stop bearing children temporarily and one to stop menstrual flow completely. There was also a plant to use to bathe the pregnant woman to stop pain. Some plants have truly medicinal qualities; some have no medicinal value but are administered in such a way as to provide legitimate nursing results. Other plants are simply valuable for the psychological effect to relieve fears and tensions associated with the symptoms. Most often, those in the latter category are plants used to work sympathetic magic, due to the size, color, or shape of the leaf, seed, bud, root or flower. One type of plant was used to bathe the pregnant woman to choose the sex of the baby to be born. The woman was bathed with the flower (*Clitoria* species) for a girl or with the small oblong fruit for a boy. One woman on the lower Aguaytia River made a trip in a dugout canoe a great distance upriver where the plant grew, to be bathed because she wanted a boy, even though she was eight months pregnant. Through the years they have lost this practice.

I also collected pictures and names of Cashibo-Cacataibo fauna: the primates (monkeys), manatees, carnivores (fox, bears, coati, jaguars, pumas), deer, anteater, sloths, armadillos, rabbits, rodents of various kinds, birds of multiple kinds, reptiles, amphibians, fish, insects, and spiders. These were also published in a booklet.

Our stay at Santa Marta was soon over and we packed our goods. We said goodbye to our Indian friends, then went back downriver, moving swiftly in the dugout canoes with a strong current carrying us

*Eight Years in the Amazon Headwaters*

along. At Puerto Inca, the plane came to pick us up and we returned to Yarinacocha base. Alice had been a good helper.

# CHAPTER 25: WITH A NURSE AS TEMPORARY PARTNER

SIL member and nurse Jo Matto was assigned to accompany me temporarily on the Lower Aguaytia for a few months. She was from the Northeast U.S. where she earned her registered nurse degree in preparation for medical ministry in the Peruvian rain forest. We packed our belongings which were loaded on the float plane. We took off from the water in nice weather bound for Mariscal Caceres on the lower Aguaytia River. After landing, we taxied over to the shore where our Cashibo friends met us and welcomed Jo. We were assigned a thatched-roof hut and unpacked our duffel bags and boxes. Soon we were settled and ready to work. Since Jo didn't know the language, I had to ask for and explain to her the symptoms of the patients. She gave the pills and/or injections, bandaged wounds, or gave treatments in general. I worked with Gregorio, the bilingual school teacher, as well as collecting and translating more narratives in the native language.

Jo was an attractive, blonde young woman who had been dating a couple of missionary men. One was in Lima, a member of another mission. He had a few radio schedules with her in the tribe. Another young man who talked with her by radio from Yarinacocha was a WBT/SIL member from the Northeast U.S.

Aside from doing medical work, Jo memorized the Cashibo words found in the first primer of primary school, as well as greetings and goodbyes. She helped by cooking meals and washing dishes, so she was busy. Even some Spanish-speaking white people came for medical treatment upon hearing there was a North American registered nurse in the village.

The months passed quickly, and we returned to Yarinacocha. Jo was soon engaged to the SIL young man, and they were later married and given another assignment together.

# CHAPTER 26: REVISING THE CASHIBO GOSPEL OF MARK

I found a rough translation of the Gospel of Mark into Cashibo-Cacataibo by Gloria Gray Wroughton and was anxious to revise it using the knowledge of the native language narrative structure learned at SIL while studying under Dr. Kenneth Pike. I spent most of 1963 and 1964 working on this project. Also, I was taking two long-distance correspondence courses of Biblical Greek during this time from the same professor of Classical Greek I had at the University of Texas at Austin. That was good preparation for Bible translation. At that time, teacher Gregorio, who had helped Gloria with her translation, was in Sungaro teaching bilingual school. I went upriver on the Aguaytia to Puerto Azul and found only Martin Cardenas available to help with the revision, since all the other men were working in their gardens or going hunting. The greatest challenge in the revision process was to make the sentences tie together in narrative form rather than translating each verse in isolation. There were also terms, such as disciples, Sabbath, synagogue, and temple in relation to the Jewish culture, which had to be translated. The term temple was translated as 'God's house' whereas synagogue was translated as 'the house (building) where the Jewish people gathered.' The term disciples was translated as 'all of Jesus' men whom he taught.' Spanish words were used for animals not found in the rain forest area, such as *camello* for camel and *burro* for donkey. After Jesus died on the cross and rose again, when Mary Magdalene, the other Mary, and other women went to the cave where Jesus was placed, the large stone was rolled away and they saw the grave clothes of Jesus. Martin asked if the cloth for Jesus' head still had His head in it. I said, "No, He was raised from the dead and the cloth was just lying there." He asked this because there are two words in Cashibo-Cacataibo for 'cloth for the head': one that is wrapped around a head and another that is for the head but is not on a head. The word for the latter was the one we wanted. The revision I made of the Gospel of Mark was completed and published in 1964. I completed my time in the tribe at the end of that year. In January of 1965, I was ill and asked to see a doctor in the United States. At that time, I packed my bags and returned to my homeland.

I missed the beauty of the rain forest: its beautiful flowers, gorgeous sunsets, wonderful tribespeople, and the interesting fauna and flora. The people of the tribes were like family to me since I had been adopted as a family member, sister to the main language consultants. They protected me and my partners from the dangers of the forest and rivers. They had great knowledge of the rain forest and how to live there. They were eager to learn that which would appeal to them. I had a skirt with many designs of feathers on it, designs copied from North American tribes. The women wanted to copy those designs in order to paint them on the hand-woven cloth they would make into skirts. Although they did not know how to read or write, they took pencil and paper I gave them and copied the designs. It was hard to leave these dear, dear tribal friends.

Flying over the rain forest had been an awe-inspiring experience. There were miles and miles of thick, uninhabited forest one could see to the east. To the west rose the green foothills with a background of majestic mountain chains followed by the dry, multicolored soil and rocks above the tree line. Although the weather below could be very hot, in the foothills there were times it took two or three layers of clothing to try to keep warm, whereas some naked little boys felt warm to the touch on the shoulder, and attested to the fact that they were not cold.

I left the tribal work in good hands, as will be seen in the Updates. However, I will never forget to pray for these three tribes and their leaders. My association with them enriched my life immensely.

# PART V: UPDATES ON THE THREE TRIBES

# CHAPTER 27: UPDATE ON THE CANDOSHI

The Shapra group of Candoshi with whom I worked, accompanying partner Lorrie Anderson, later moved back up to the Pushaga River from which they had fled when Chief Tariri was seriously wounded and one man killed in a revenge killing. Everyone knew that Tariri was not going to retaliate since he had become a Christian. Being a leading war chief, Tariri's refusal to revenge an attempt on his life proved to be the wedge which broke the apparently unbreakable cycle of Candoshi warfare (S. Tuggy, 1985:29).

Chief Tariri's son, Tsirimpo, had been handicapped by a foot condition which made him walk on his tiptoes since his muscles and bones were frozen into that position. Someone contacted Mayo Clinic doctors in Minnesota about the possibility of straightening Tsirimpo's feet. They accepted the challenge and Tsirimpo, accompanied by nurse Mary Beth Hinson, flew to the Mayo Clinic to have surgery on his feet. The doctors operated and it was successful—his feet were leveled so that they allowed him to walk flat on the ground and to wear shoes. He was ecstatic. Tsirimpo studied Spanish and was trained to become a bilingual teacher in the Shapra family group of Candoshi on the Pushaga River. Shirimpo, another young man, also became a Shapra bilingual teacher. Later, other Candoshi men were trained and bilingual schools established on the following rivers: the Sicuanga (a tributary of the Morona River), and the Chapori and Chovinta Rivers which flow into Rimachi Lake. New communities are beginning just about every year on these rivers. Tsirimpo died in the early 1980's. Irina, Tariri's wife, died in 1992 and Tariri died around the year 1994.

Lorrie continued working on New Testament translation though she had to return to New Jersey numerous times in the seventies because of the ill health of one or another of her family. Over a period of time she translated the Epistles to the Colossians and Romans, and various other epistles, as well as the Gospel of John. In 1978 she took part in the final revision of the Candoshi New Testament, along with the Tuggys. In October of 1980 she returned to the United States to care for her elderly mother who was ill. In 1981 she was invited to the JAARS Center in Waxhaw, North Carolina, to work in the recruitment of new translators living in the Carolinas. JAARS is Wycliffe's international center for technological support, including information technology, aviation, vernacular media and computer work. Lorrie and her mother moved from New Jersey to North Carolina. She then spent her time speaking to audiences in colleges and universities seeking to challenge them with stories of the Candoshis. She also spoke in many churches about her work. Lorrie was later assigned to writing, and was on the staff of Intercultural Communications Course for new missionaries for a number of years. Every few years she was able to go to Peru for short visits of about eight weeks at a time to be with the Candoshi in one or more villages and minister to them. In 1994 she went to Peru for nine months to record more than half of the New Testament in Candoshi along with John and four native speakers. She and an old friend, Gracie Torres, were able to go out for six weeks visiting Chief Tariri and others.

In 1959 John and Sheila Tuggy were assigned to work on the Candoshi translation of the New Testament. Although the Shapra men had said they would have killed Lorrie and Doris had they been men, after Chief Tariri and others had become Christians, they liked the white men pilots and other men they had encountered at Yarinacocha. Therefore, when the Tuggys were assigned to their tribe, the Shapra men were very happy to have a man to deal with. John had grown up in Venezuela with missionary parents. He was fluent in English and Spanish. His wife Sheila, whom he met at SIL, was a slim, blonde young woman from Scotland. They had four children to raise: Joy, Ruth, June, and Bob. Aside from that great responsibility, their first job was to learn the Candoshi language, not an easy task, but one for which they had excellent linguistic training at SIL. I had some classes in linguistics with John at the University of Oklahoma SIL.

The Tuggys learned the Candoshi phonology (sound system) and John wrote grammar notes of the Candoshi language from time to time, which he presented to his supervisor, who then filed them away. They had to know these topics to gain permission for translating the New Testament. There were commentaries in English of some books of Scripture, called "Translator's Notes on Mark," or to whichever book of the Bible they referred. These were a great help in presenting ideas of how to translate as they came out year by year.

The books of the Candoshi New Testament had been printed up one by one, as translated, and so were in the hands of the people to read. The Tuggys translated the rest of the books of the New Testament into Candoshi. The complete Candoshi New Testament was published in 1979 and dedicated in 1980. Once it was completed and available in one volume, the Candoshi pastors were delighted to be able to preach from it more easily. The pastors had been trained at the Swiss Indian Mission Bible School.

After the New Testament was completed, groups of believers sprang up in communities where there were bilingual schools. Further up the Pastaza River on small tributaries there are also Candoshi believers now. There are no bilingual schools there. The children are taught in the Spanish language by teachers from the cities. Even so, the children learn to read easily in Candoshi also.

"The Candoshi world consists of two realms: the lower world of forest, rivers, mountains (*tsaporonasi*)... and the upper world above the earth (*kaninta*).... Our Father (*apanchi*) has his home in the upper world; but no one knows what he sees there.... Candoshi mythological history can be divided into two eras—that in which Father frequently appeared in the lower world, and the present era in which he still has an interest in helping people but no longer appears in visible form." (Tuggy 1985:8,9,10) "From the beginning the people identified the God of the Bible as Our Father." (Tuggy 1985:28) As such, he was chosen to be God in the Bible translations. He wanted good for the Candoshi with such values as kindness, happiness, truthfulness, and honesty. "Acts considered bad (*yotarita*) include violent behavior in general, incest, adultery, premarital sexual relations, hate and its manifestations, anger, and stealing. Killing is 'bad', but it was considered right to avenge a death." (Tuggy 1985:9) "Although good and evil were well defined by the Candoshi, for the greater majority of men there was no compulsion to focus on the 'good' aspects of life.... Spirit power, which promised life preservation, goaded men to kill. Having killed, they lived in constant fear of revenge, which generated more killing." (Tuggy 1985:27,28)

Once the New Testament was completed and dedicated, the Candoshi pastors who were trained at the Swiss Bible School could preach from the New Testament in their own language. In the year 2000, something significant happened. The Shapras formed an association of churches and appointed leaders to arrange Bible conferences and a Bible training center. The Candoshi believers have had an association of churches and had already been organizing conferences and Bible training centers for over ten years, but until this time, the Shapras never seemed to be able to cooperate and move ahead. A group of younger people was the catalyst in that movement. They did not set the older pastors aside, but voted some of them into positions of leadership.

As found in the New Testament, "that Father's son had come to the world to give his life as a propitiatory sacrifice for the evil of mankind, that he was resurrected from death and now offered eternal life to those who would accept his sacrifice was a significant change from the traditional story of Father's son in Candoshi mythology.... The issue now became a choice between following the way of Father or the way of the evil spirits." (Tuggy 1985:28) Due to Biblical teaching, widows and orphans are treated better by Christians. Christian men do not beat their wives, but are taught to love them as they love themselves. Christians do not practice infanticide. Even as Christians "the two highest social values continue to be as before (1) the self-reliance of the adult male, and (2) loyalty to family. All Candoshi life revolves around these two values." (Tuggy 1985:36)

In the year 2000, the Candoshi were front-page news in one of Lima's leading newspapers. The sad article reported on the number of Candoshi who had died of hepatitis in the past few years. The article called on the new government, which had just been inaugurated, to help them with medicines and hepatitis vaccine. Hepatitis has been a longstanding problem among the Candoshi and began to reach epidemic proportions during the eighties. Medical teams had twice vaccinated some people, but there had never been a consistent vaccination program. In 2003 the World Health Organization went in and vaccinated all children three years old and under. They gave refrigerators to the *Sanitarios* (medically trained Candoshi) in which to keep vaccine so they could vaccinate newborns. The most recent vaccinations were given only to children three years old and under. The health officials said it was useless to do otherwise. Nothing could be done for children over three, or for adults, especially if they already had hepatitis. Hepatitis B is the most prevalent there, and it is deadly, especially in combination with the malignant cerebral malaria also endemic in the area, falciparum.

The people also wanted to have the Old Testament in their language to complete the whole Bible in Candoshi. This was a challenge to John and Sheila. In March of 2001, they wanted at least two Candoshi speakers to go to Pucallpa to work on the Old Testament translation. Just the year before, the Spanish translation of "Translator's Notes on Luke" (over 700 pages) was off the press, and other New Testament books were in preparation. John was leading a team of translators involved in producing these Bible commentaries for translators living in Spanish-speaking countries. They would be used by the bilingual Candoshi mother-tongue translators to prepare first drafts of Old Testament books.

From July seventh to September third of 2001, the Tuggys spent time in Peru with the main purpose of training Candoshi speakers to translate the Old Testament from Spanish. The actual workshop time was eight weeks with three participants: Oroshpa Totarica, Powanchi Tayanta, and Mariano Okama. Oroshpa had about a third grade primary education, plus several years at the Swiss Indian Mission Bible School, and many years of experience teaching the Bible to the Candoshi in their language. Powanchi, who had completed his Spanish high school education, was quite intelligent, and worked quickly. However, he had hepatitis complicated by a drug resistant variety of falciparum malaria. Mariano had about fourth grade primary education and had fair contact with Spanish speakers. His ability in Spanish, however, was too limited to continue in the drafting stage of the translation process, but did very well at the reviewing and correcting stage.

The Tuggys experimented, using various types of materials to see which they could best understand and use. They ended up using the United Bible Society's Spanish Popular Version (VP) written in a simple language style. The translators managed to complete Genesis chapters one through twenty and about eight Psalms. Powanchi had the assignment to complete Genesis in rough draft, and Oroshpa to rough draft selected parts of Exodus. Their total objective was to translate 40% of the Old Testament, which included most of the background knowledge alluded to in the New Testament and a few other parts that were of interest. This 40% selection was made and recommended by the United Bible Society.

Radio programs of Candoshi New Testament readings had been ready to be aired for two years, but no one had seen the matter through to having them aired over some commercial radio station near the Candoshi. John tried to find a radio station with someone to make certain the programs would be aired daily, and is still seeking some consistent, inexpensive way to get funds to the station. These programs are still not being aired. The problem is finding a station which beams into the Candoshi area that would be willing to air the programs.

In time past, the Tuggys had prepared selected Psalms for the Candoshi to translate, but Sheila had wanted to prepare more of the Psalms. As a preliminary step, she studied some of the Candoshi stories in the files and also reviewed the grammar materials in the files. They had been working on Old Testament translation at Cashibococha near Pucallpa. After being in the United States for a while and with their advancing age, Sheila and John discovered that they could no longer physically tolerate the extreme heat and humidity in the rain forest. To even think of continuing the Candoshi Old Testament translation project required a much cooler environment.

SIL would be leaving Yarinacocha and turning the base over to the Peruvian government to be the location of a university for tribal students. The Tuggys wanted to locate farther north to be nearer the Candoshi tribe, which is about 300 feet above sea level, and in a steamy jungle. They went to Moyobamba, the capital of the Province of San Martin at an elevation of 2500 feet, as a location where they could be in a cooler climate and live comfortably in an inexpensive house while working on the Old Testament translation. They also had to secure housing for the three Candoshi translators and their families, but they did not have the money for it outside of the project budget. At first they rented a house, but then they found a house for the three Candoshi families which cost only a little more than $3,000. The Lord laid it on the heart of one of Lorrie Anderson's cousins in California to help the project financially, and he provided all the funds needed for that purchase. The house was named Candoshi House.

John arranged with SIM missionaries to send his cargo from Pucallpa to Moyobamba safely. In the fall of 2003, there was a series of flights returning students from many different language groups to their homes after completing a year of training at SIM's Bible School. The flights from Candoshi-land were returning totally empty. John requested that the Candoshi translators and their families be flown directly to Moyobamba. This was done, bringing the three families from their doorsteps to the doorsteps of the Candoshi House.

The vegetation at Moyobamba is like that of Pucallpa, but the elevation is a little higher and the climate is not as humid as in the lowland rain forest. It does not have the same searing, damp heat as Pucallpa. In the shade, there is a bit of breeze that gives a coolness to the air. The folk there call it the *selva* (rain forest). The three Candoshi mother-tongue translators and their families were all suffering from culture shock in the city. They hated to have to buy firewood when it was free back home. Also, they were not happy to pay *mototaxi* fares everywhere they went. But that was life around town. The folk in the Presbyterian Church, who helped the Tuggys locate there, were wonderful. The church provided a classroom where the translators could work without distraction. Four of the Candoshi children were registered in the Presbyterian school for a four week summer course to help them learn some Spanish, at least enough to communicate with the children on the street around them. One of the ladies in the church worked with the three Candoshi women to make patterns and sew clothing while the children were in school. Victor, the man who helped John greatly with housing, was a neighbor from the church. He took all the Candoshi out to his cousin's fields one day. They pulled up enough manioc root to make their drink. Then he took them to a lake to look for fish. They didn't catch any fish, but they did get some large water snails and were delighted with them. Seeing how happy they were with them, he took them to some rice fields where there were many of a smaller variety of snails. The farmers don't like the snails because they eat the rice, so they were extremely happy to have the Candoshi wade among the rice and gather the snails. They invited them back whenever they wanted to come for more.

The translation was moving along well. Oroshpa had finished entering on computer the suggestions in Exodus which the people in his village made when he checked it with them. The last half of Genesis was ready for the final review. Right after that, the final polish of Exodus would be done. Powanchi had been working on First Samuel and Juan on First Kings. Their new technique was to read the passage over several times in Spanish, and then, once they had it firmly in mind, they recorded it and transcribed it onto the computer. It took a bit longer, but seemed to make a much smoother translation. Oroshpa also started using this technique for drafting the short book of Ezra. Juan and Powanchi took a computer course at a local technical school three nights a week for three months.

After September 11, 2001, donations to WBT/SIL for projects dropped off dramatically. In March of 2003, the Tuggys saw one Old Testament translation project in Peru come to a screeching halt for lack of funds. The three mother-tongue translators asked, "Will our project stop, too?" John explained that the funds were in hand to complete Phase Two of the Candoshi Old Testament. Again he was asked, "Well, will there be funds to continue next year?" John answered, "We don't know. But if $5,000 has arrived by the time you go home at the end of May, you will know that we will continue. Will you be willing to continue working without any pay? We would just cover your travel, food, and medical bills." There was a long silence. "Yes, we will trust the Lord for what is needed," they said. By the time the translators went home, there were NO FUNDS! They went home not knowing if the project would continue. But they said, "We will work on the translation while we are home, because if we do not, we will never finish!"

The Tuggys returned to the U.S. not knowing if they would be able to continue. Later they found out that some of their long-time supporters had sent $5,000 for the Old Testament project, but the funds had been misdirected and did not get into the project fund until later. Then another $5,000 was promised for the fourth phase of the Old Testament translation.

John returned to Peru, but Sheila needed to stay and wait for her naturalization for U.S. citizenship. She waited until she received notice that she would complete the naturalization process by being sworn in on November 14. Only the Lord could have orchestrated this arrangement, as they had thought it might take three months for the government to move on the naturalization. She waited only two months for her passport until she joined John in Peru after all.

In the fall of 2003, John turned "three score years and ten (70)." His dad said, "Every day is borrowed time." Even so, he and Sheila do not intend to retire for a few more years yet. They want to at least finish helping the Candoshi translators complete the Old Testament translation project, which should be at least another four years. As long as God gives them minds, will, energy, and health, they want to keep journeying on.

In 2004, at the age of 81, Lorrie Anderson made a trip to Peru visiting Peruvian and Candoshi friends in Lima, Moyobamba, and Pucallpa. She took with her the fifteen episodes on the video titled *The Complete Life of Christ* from the Gospel of Luke with audio recording in the Candoshi language. The video is four and one-half hours long, therefore not shown at one sitting, but one episode at a time (twenty to thirty minutes each) along with a Bible study on that passage. The videos had been in production since 1998. Lorrie prepared the video with the help of Louise Derr, the Vernacular Media Services trainer from JAARs Center, who accompanied her to Peru. Six Candoshi men had been trained to show the video in thirty scattered communities. They were also trained to repair the video-playing machines. While in Moyobamba, Lorrie and Louise showed some of the videos to the three Candoshi mother-tongue translators and their families who were excited about them. There are two sets of video-playing equipment, which are heavy. They hope to replace them with the lighter twenty-one-pound back-pack players

*Updates on the Three Tribes*

for DVD's. Many more are needed for the thirty communities. The villages are scattered on different rivers, which are hours or days apart in the rain forest. There are no roads, so travel is still by river. Lorrie continues to pray for the Tuggys and the Candoshi people.

# CHAPTER 28: UPDATE ON THE AGUARUNA

Within the last four decades, a significant sequence of culture change has taken place among the Aguaruna people, most numerous member of the Jivaro family of languages in Peru. These culture changes considerably alter the picture of Jivaro head-shrinking culture painted by early historical, scientific, and semifictional books. Behind the changes lie two chief factors in what has become a directed, nativistic movement to aid Aguarunas in their struggle for continuity as a tribe. Those factors are: (1) the Aguaruna and Spanish bilingual school, and (2) acceptance of Christianity by a great number of Aguaruna. The bilingual schools were sponsored jointly by the Peruvian Ministry of Education and SIL. A third factor which greatly effected change was the road which came through their area bringing many white people and Western civilization right to their doorstep.

Aguaruna study hall at Yarinacocha base bilingual school teacher training

From a handful of men teaching in the 1950's, by 1967 the number of teachers had increased to 88 and now it is up well over one hundred. The cumulative effects of the system produced a basis for tribal unity. Today the Aguarunas have their own print shop where they prepare books for the many schools now in existence. They even have a computer in their print shop. In one generation they have moved from illiteracy into the electronic age.

There have been culture changes in the areas of education, politics, law, territorial settlement, and economics. All through these general spheres runs the pervading influence of the bilingual school as an institutionalized, shared component between Aguaruna culture and Spanish-speaking Western culture. It has acted as a buffer between the two cultures to maintain proper balance. This delicate balance requires the backing of the Peruvian government in land problems against the overwhelming weight of power on the side of the white people to keep away anxiety and hostile actions. So far, the Aguarunas have had rather peaceful acculturation. Other missions, both Catholic and Protestant, saw the positive effects of the bilingual schools and established their own bilingual schools. Their earlier schools had emphasized need for complete rejection of Aguaruna cultural practices and total acceptance of the Spanish language and Western culture. They had come to realize that it is best to learn to read first in one's own language and then their second language, Spanish. Under the previous system, no outstanding leaders or nativistic movements were produced to effect bilingualism and culture change, keeping what was good in the Aguaruna culture and the national culture.

Missionary attempts to learn and analyze the Aguaruna language were hindered by lack of linguistic and anthropological orientation until the arrival of members of SIL in 1946. I worked with the Aguarunas in 1956, 1957 and 1958. With Millie Larson and then Jeanne Grover, we were preparing the people for the changes to come and training to prepare the Aguarunas for the advance of the east-west road that would link the Pan American highway on the coast with interior points through and beyond Aguaruna rain forest-covered territory. The dirt and then gravel highway has become part of a network of roads proposed to connect the future north-south marginal highway on the eastern side of the Andes in order to open up new areas for settlement and exploitation by whites. For many years, Aguarunas anticipated with fear the advance of this road with its accompanying problems of increased white population. At first, the "old ones" panicked and wanted to retreat to the hills, but proposals by SIL members for positive steps to counteract the problems convinced tribal elders and bilingual teachers of the efficacy to remain on occupied territory. The road construction began in Nazaret in 1966 and proceeded through the east to below Borja around 1976. Whites moved in and planted trees producing the tropical fruit *coconas* and pineapple plants, but when it rained, the road was a sea of mud. They couldn't get their produce to market and went bankrupt. At first, whites tried planting on Indian land, but the Aguarunas were able to follow lawful procedures to get many whites off their land.

In the past, outsiders coming into Aguaruna country saw vast expanses of virgin jungle and they were appalled at all that land going to waste. But the forests are very important to the original Aguaruna economy. Each home needs one or two trees a week for firewood, more or less 150 trees a year for one village. Besides the firewood, they need 3,500 palm leaves for each house roof, four to eight foundation posts, and many trees for beams and rafters. The village needs from one to five school houses, a clinic house, and a store. All of this represents a fantastic number of leaves, as well as a great amount of vine to tie them all together (Grover 1970:3).

The coming of the road through their area has changed their settlement pattern. In order to secure their tribal territory, instead of living in scattered, loosely-knit, family groups, they now live in better-defined, larger groups with required political organization. Patrilineal reckoning and patrilocal residence remain the general pattern. Previously, polygyny was relatively prevalent, but now they are aware of the national law of monogamy, as well as discovering the biblical teaching of monogamy.

At 5 a.m. the Aguaruna young men in one village were awakened by the village loud speaker. "It's now five o'clock," announced the Aguaruna Christian pastor, and then read a passage of Scripture in Aguaruna language and prayed. This was a cultural substitute for

*Updates on the Three Tribes*

the old custom of getting everyone up early so the elders could teach the young people about hating their enemies, revenge, and killing. Now they are taught to love one another, including their enemies. (information from Dennis Olson)

The Aguarunas numbered about 20,000 in the 1950's, living on scattered hill-tops located in northwestern Peru in the eastern foothills of the Andes Mountains. Their territory covered about one hundred square miles along the Marañon River and its affluents between Nazaret and Morona. Presently, the tribal population number has doubled to 40,000. Medical treatment saves lives and has prolonged life. They are no longer killing each other in revenge killings, much of this attributed to the fact that many have become Christians by their own choice and made peace with their enemies through interacting together in their education. Nazaret was just a small community when I was there, but by the 1990's the population there was 1,250. The people could no longer hunt to get meat because there was not enough game. Sometimes they have had only cans of tuna or chicken to eat.

An Aguaruna-owned store

The SIL, along with the Peruvian government, had special courses to prepare the Aguaruna for the changes when the road would come through their area. Men were trained in mechanics with a goal of enabling them to repair motors and get spare parts, particularly for motor boats. They were helped in getting community boats, so they could take their produce to market. The Aguaruna men were trained in carpentry to help them get tools of the trade and to know how to use them. They were also trained to install and use small sawmills so that they could build their houses, stores, and schools using lumber. They were given cattle and taught how to take care of their herds. They were given good breeding stock of cattle, hogs, and chickens. They were trained and helped to establish stores, so they would not be solely dependent on white traders who had previously charged them many times what the trade goods were worth in the early years when the volume of trade exceeded the calculating abilities of the Aguaruna. Matches, flashlights with their batteries, soap, brooms, fish hooks and lines, as well as other basic supplies can now be bought in their own stores. They also had a small rice-hulling machine and a rice winnower. Rice is one of their main products grown for sale to the outside world. In 1970, Jeanne began the training and supervision of Aguaruna health promoters. With the help of a microscope, she was able to show the living microbes in the water, convincing many people to boil their water.

Aguarunas had a small rice hulling machine

Martha Jakway, an SIL woman trained in education, was assigned in 1964 to work with the Aguaruna bilingual schools since they had become so numerous. As there had been a married couple assigned to the Candoshi, there was also a married couple, Dennis and Susy Olson, assigned to the Aguaruna. The Olsons concentrated on helping the Aguarunas cope with culture change and social problems. These workers freed Mildred Larson for the New Testament translation. Even so, for a while she was making slow progress on the translation due to the many problems which arose from the coming of the road through the area.

Near Nazaret at Chiriaco, there was a mission, all-Spanish school with modern buildings and playground equipment as well as free food and clothing for the students. At first, many children left their bilingual schools to attend the new modern school, but eventually many returned to their bilingual schools because they missed their language, their own tribal food, and their own Aguaruna scriptures and songs which had been translated thus far. To further the translation project, Alias helped Millie with translation for a while, but, in 1966, took a leave of absence from teaching to help translate the book of Acts. After that was finished, Alias made a missionary trip to Aguaruna areas where there were no churches and the gospel was not known. Later, Millie worked with Nelson Pujupat as co-translator. He had been taught at the Bible School of the Swiss Indian Mission. After Millie taught him principles of translation, they worked on translating I Thessalonians. Millie also taught him how to type on a typewriter so that he could type up his own translations in that period before computers. They worked for several years until July 26, 1971, when, together, Millie and Nelson translated the last verse of the book of Revelation into Aguaruna language. Nelson had also studied four years at a Bible school in the Andes Mountains (not sponsored by the Swiss Indian Mission), giving him further background for understanding the New Testament in Spanish and aiding him in transferring concepts to Aguaruna. After the initial translation, there were several years of checking it to be sure that it was accurate. Then it had to be laid out and printed. Finally, the translated New Testament in the Aguaruna language arrived in Nazaret on October 14, 1975. There were 10,000 books in boxes that

*Eight Years in the Amazon Headwaters*

would be sent to a hundred other Aguaruna communities (Larson & Dodds1985:270). There was then a twelve-day celebration to cover fifteen villages attended by SIL workers Millie, Martha, Jeanne, Dennis, and nurse Joy Congdon. Co-translators Alias and Nelson also joined in. Even at Nieva, a mestizo community, the priests and nuns had a celebration in a packed church. Father Pancho asked the Aguarunas to do three things: to read the Aguaruna New Testament, meditate on it, and pray. Sister Juliana read John 17, emphasizing Jesus' prayer that his followers would be one. Catholic and Protestant brothers and sisters in Christ were present, united in presenting the Aguaruna New Testament to the people (Larson 1985:274).

As the years went by, the Aguaruna New Testament was taught and preached in over one hundred villages. Since they lived closer together, the need of God's love for one another and for the white people bordering their area was taught. Scriptural truths helped the Christians have patience and even tempers in the midst of culture change. Finally, at the turn of the millennium, the need for a revision was felt. Dr. Mildred Larson had left Peru and earned her Ph.D. to help her in various executive jobs at the International Linguistic Center (ILC) in Dallas. She later retired to her home area of Minnesota to write one last book to help others in translating. She continues to keep contact with the Aguaruna and to pray for them.

In 2002, the revision of the Aguaruna New Testament was undertaken by mother-tongue translators with Stan Schauer as consultant. He did not know the Aguaruna language but worked with the translators through Spanish as they back-translated their revisions of the Aguaruna New Testament into Spanish and discussed it with him. The two primary revisers were Marcial Petsavit and Isaias Daati. They would each spend a month out in their village working on the revision and checking the material with other members of the community. Then they would go to the SIL center for about three weeks for consultant help, keying their revisions on the computer. Finally, they completed revising the whole New Testament in 2004.

Following the revision of the New Testament, as in the Candoshi tribe, the Aguarunas also began work on the Old Testament, translated by mother-tongue translators and then checked by a Wycliffe person. After the Candoshi left Moyobamba in 2004 to go to their tribal locations to review what they had translated, the Aguaruna Old Testament translators went to Moyobamba to work on checking their translated material in the Presbyterian Church as the Candoshi had done. This work on the Aguaruna Old Testament continues.

# CHAPTER 29: UPDATE ON THE CACATAIBO WORK

The Panoan people of the Aguaytia and Sungaroyacu Rivers had been called by the name Cashibo, a name meaning "Vampire Bat People," a name that they never liked. The people on the San Alejandro River were called Cacataibo, a name that did not have negative connotation. As time went on and the millennium turned, the decision was made to call the whole tribe on all three rivers "Cacataibo".

After I went home on sick leave, I saw some medical doctors and improved in health. I went back to the University of Texas at Austin to complete my degrees, finishing my B.A., M.A., and Ph.D. with a double major in linguistics and folklore, the folklore being credited as anthropology along with my other anthropology courses. My dissertation was a presentation of nineteen myths and tales of Cacataibo with folkloric analysis and linguistic summary along with translations of the stories. I received my Ph.D. in August of 1969.

After Dr. Olive Shell returned to Peru, she had a heart attack at the base and was in serious condition for some time. She became progressively weaker and came to the point that she was so weak that she could not even push the button to call the base medical doctor. People all over the base were praying for her. The executive committee, a group of three or four men, decided to follow the model of James 5:14-15a in the Bible: "Is any sick among you? Let him [or her] call for the elders of the church, and let them pray over [her], anointing [her] with oil in the name of the Lord; and the prayer of faith shall save the sick, and the Lord shall raise [her] up...." The directors went to Olive's bedside at the base clinic, anointed her with oil, and prayed fervently that God would heal her. From that moment on, she rallied and began to gain strength. With time she had a complete recovery and had no other heart trouble for the rest of her life. She did not immediately return to the Cashibo-Cacataibo work. She filled an executive position with the bilingual schools at the base, partly because she had been a teacher in Canada before

*Updates on the Three Tribes*

joining WBT/SIL. Her health improved until she was returned to normal strength.

After recovering from her heart attack, a healthy Olive began the job of translating the whole New Testament into the Cacataibo language. She worked with co-translator Gregorio Estrella Odicio, who had the best command of Spanish language due to his years of service to the Peruvian army in Lima, in addition to a good background in his own language. The whole New Testament was completed in 1977 and distributed to people on all three rivers. Dedication was in December of 1978 when Dr. Shell, James and Gloria Wroughton, and Lois Dodds went out to the Lower Aguaytia for a small ceremony. In mid-1987, Olive retired to Dallas at the International Linguistic Center to be editor of *Notes on Literacy* until early 1992. At that time in her 80's, she retired to Canada and died on November 24, 1994. She had accomplished much in her lifetime.

Gerhard and Martha Ritter from Germany, who worked with the Swiss Indian Mission (SIM), were fluent in Spanish and also became very fluent in the Cacataibo language. Gerhard had trained some of the young men from the tribe at the SIM Bible School, where he also later became Director. He helped the Cacataibo young men to become pastors and to establish six churches in the tribe. These churches became members of FAIENAP (*Federación de Iglesias Evangelicas Nativas de la Amazonia Peruana*) which is, in English, the Federation of Native Evangelical Churches of the Peruvian Amazon. Gerhard went out to teach and encourage the pastors and church members.

During the time of the Ritters' work with the Cacataibo, the Shining Path revolutionary guerillas invaded the tribal areas. The Shining Path members wanted to kill native people who would not cooperate with them as well as outsiders such as the Ritters. Once when Gerhard was out on the San Alejandro River, the Indians heard the loud noise of a motorboat full of the guerillas nearing them upriver. The Cacataibo took Gerhard deep into the forest to hide him. The guerillas arrived and looked all around for Gerhard for several days, but never found him, so finally left. It was a close call.

Later, both Gerhard and Martha were going to fly to a downriver Aguaytia location. They were all packed and ready to board the plane when Martha had extreme pains in her heart and had to be taken to the medical doctor in Pucallpa. Their flight was cancelled. Later, they learned that government troops had a terrible gun battle with Shining Path members right where the Ritters would have landed had they gone. God saved their lives. Many men were killed in the gunfight.

In August of 1998, Gerhard completed a hymn book in Cacataibo. It was published by the SIM and greatly appreciated by the six churches. Soon after, the Ritters had to leave Peru and return to Germany due to serious health problems. A middle-aged *mestizo* named Romualdo Moreno Ipushima living in Pucallpa was sponsored by SIM to take the place of Gerhard Ritter. Pucallpa was just a small city of a couple thousand people when I was there, but now is a rapidly growing city with a population of approximately 200,000. Romualdo had a small Christian bookstore and sold musical instruments in Pucallpa. His wife would take over in the store when Romualdo began going out to Cacataibo locations to teach the Bible to the pastors and church members. He did not know the Cacataibo language, but taught them Bible lessons and sang hymns and choruses with them in Spanish at meetings where all six pastors met together at one location along with other believers. The youth and children began to prefer the teaching in Spanish, but there was always a translator for those who preferred their native language. Romualdo had a computer with an email address and began to email correspondence with me in Spanish for several years. He would receive money from me taken by a friend now living in the U.S. who was a Peruvian who grew up in Pucallpa. The money was used by Cacataibo who needed to see a medical doctor and/or eye doctor in Pucallpa with Romualdo's help. Romualdo no longer works with the Cacataibo, therefore, I no longer get reports on their activities. There is now a telephone at Puerto Azul on the Upper Aguaytia River. Also, the government is now giving televisions to tribal people so that they can keep up with what is going on in their nation. Times have really changed.

The revision of the Cacataibo New Testament was completed by mother-tongue translators in 1995. Presently, they are working on the Old Testament translation with help from WBT workers under the FAINEAP Mother-Tongue Project. It is designed to train and assist sixteen mother-tongue translators to provide 40% of the Old Testament in six jungle languages, including Cacataibo. Many of the mother-tongue translators were lacking in computer and Spanish as a Second Language skills. They received tutoring in these subjects twice a week from mid-2004 until December of 2004. Many of the Cacataibo becoming Christians has almost ended revenge killing and the feelings of animosity between groups.

Yarinacocha base of SIL/WBT is no longer their base of operations. It is in the planning stage of becoming UNIA (*Universidad Nacional Intercultural de Amazonas*), the National Intercultural University of the Amazon in English. This will be a university for the benefit of the native people of Peru, particularly for bilingual school teachers to get their advanced education.

# *EPILOGUE*

The Lord graciously placed me in a middle-class, Christian home with parents who loved God and were good role models. I was the middle child of five siblings. Born in Chicago, I moved to Houston, Texas, with my family when I was eight years old. We all experienced culture shock in this southern location where we were called Yankees and told that we talked differently. To my consternation, the Houston second graders had learned to read and write longhand, whereas I had only learned to print in second grade in Chicago. When the third grade teacher in Houston wrote longhand on the blackboard, I burst into tears. This was one of the adjustments to be made.

In 1940, we moved outside of Houston to the Almeda area, moving into a home built by my maternal grandfather on five acres of land donated by my paternal grandfather. During World War II, due to gasoline rationing, we decided to join Minnetex Community Church, which was only three miles from our home out on the flat prairie of the Gulf coast. Minnetex had many missionary speakers. I had responded to the Gospel teachings at Camp Peniel, a Christian camp in the Sam Houston National Forest north of Houston, and to the Minnetex pastor's invitation to accept Christ as my personal Savior, paving the way for future missionary work.

After receiving my Ph.D. in 1969, I was hired as Assistant Professor of Linguistics and Anthropology at Kansas State University (KSU) in Manhattan, Kansas, to begin teaching in the fall semester of that year. I was on leave of absence from SIL/WBT during this time. My father, Elmer Wistrand, in Houston, Texas, had terminal colon cancer. I wanted to stay in the States during this time and also wanted to have some experience teaching before returning to Peru. My father died October 14, 1969, and I flew to Houston for his funeral. The next year I taught again at KSU, during which time I met Dr. Albert Robinson who lived in Assaria, Kansas, and taught biology and botany at Kansas Wesleyan University in Salina, Kansas. He was fluent in Spanish, having taken botany trips to Mexico and also earned a Fulbright grant to serve in Bucaramanga, Colombia, at

*La Universidad Industrial de Santander*. He had visited SIL/WBT centers in Mexico and Colombia and so was acquainted with my mission. He was just at the point of changing jobs, having been hired by the Kansas Department of Agriculture Weed and Pesticide Division in Topeka at the end of the university school year. We met in 1970 and were married July 31, 1971. Having married someone outside of the mission, I was no longer a member of SIL/WBT. I taught at KSU one more year during our first year of marriage, then we moved to Topeka where Albert's job was.

During my last year of teaching, I had a small grant to study the Iowa-Otoe language of Native Americans living in Kansas and Oklahoma, with the help of a graduate student at KSU. My student traveled to Topeka to interview and tape record the language of an Iowa woman after I prepared the word list for her. Then I prepared a vocabulary list for the tribal language. Following this, with the help of Jimm Good Tracks of Oklahoma, we received grants for me to prepare two books to document the language so that younger people could learn the Iowa-Otoe language. I would go to Oklahoma for one week of a month to work with older people who spoke the language fluently, then worked on preparing pages to teach the language the rest of the month. I did this for a couple of years until the two books were completed. The books were titled *Jiwele-Baxoje Wan'shige Ukenye Ich'e*: Otoe-Iowa Indian Language, Books I and II, published in 1977 and 1978, respectively.

Later, I received a grant from National Endowment for the Humanities (NEH Project 1366) to prepare a dictionary from a shoebox of yellowed 3x5 slips, which were the collection of Comanche words elicited by Elliott Canonge of SIL in the 1940's. The grant came through KSU, so I asked linguist Dr. James Armagost to work with me by preparing the grammar section of the book. I took eight week-long trips to Oklahoma over a fourteen-month period during 1978 and 1979 to check approximately 3,500 words with the Comanche language consultants. From these consultations, the dictionary was prepared and sent to SIL to computerize and publish. Finally, in 1990 the *Comanche Dictionary and Grammar* was published. In working on the Comanche language, I decided that there was a linguistic relationship between Cashibo-Cacataibo and Comanche. I wrote and published also in 1990 an article titled "Uto-Aztecan affinities with Panoan of Peru I: Correspondences."

After finishing the Comanche dictionary, I decided to take many of the myths and tales of my Ph.D. dissertation, add to them, and include a culture sketch of the Cashibo tribe (before the name was changed to Cacataibo). I prepared fifty-two examples of prose and ten examples of song poetry. The book was then titled *Cashibo Folklore and Culture*: Prose, Poetry, and Historical Background, published in 1998 by SIL in Dallas, Texas.

From Kansas, in 1978, my husband and I moved to Lynchburg, Virginia to teach full-time at Liberty Baptist College, which became Liberty University while we were there. I taught cultural anthropology, cross-cultural communications, and linguistics to students who planned to go overseas to be missionaries under a variety of missions. We taught there for nine years, then both retired from full-time teaching. I have continued correspondence with many of these students as they have been working in many countries around the world, thankful for their courses in anthropology and linguistics.

In 1987 we moved to part-time teaching in Walnut Ridge, Arkansas, to be near my mother-in-law who was located sixty miles away in the little town of Franklin. She passed away in 1988 at ninety and one-half years. We both taught at Southern Baptist College (SBC), a two-year college, for three years. In 1990 I became ill and dropped out of teaching for a year. My husband continued teaching at SBC, which became a four-year college named Williams Baptist College (WBC). Dr. Albert taught there for fourteen years until retirement. I resumed teaching in January of 1992 for Arkansas State University (ASU) at Black River Technical College (BRTC) for a year and a half. Then when BRTC gained accreditation as a two-year college I remained teaching cultural anthropology and sociology, a total of ten years under ASU and BRTC, until retirement.

# *BIBLIOGRAPHY*

Eakin, Lucille, Erwin Lauriault, and Harry Boonstra. 1986. *People of the Ucayali: The Shipibo and Conibo of Peru.* Dallas: Summer Institute of Linguistics and the International Museum of Cultures Publications in Ethnography.

Grover, Jeanne. 1970. "Land Development Among the Aguarunas: The Indians' needs in relation to the land." Unpublished manuscript.

Gray Wroughton, Gloria. 1953. "Bolivar Odicio, el cashibo civilizador." *Perú Indígena* 4 (9): 146-54.

Larson, Mildred. 1975. *A Manual for Problem Solving in Bible Translation.* Dallas: Summer Institute of Linguistics, 245 pp.

Larson, Mildred L. and Patricia M. Davis. 1981. *Bilingual Education: An Experience in Peruvian Amazonia.* Dallas: Summer Institute of Linguistics, 417 pp.

Larson, Mildred and Lois Dodds. 1985. *Treasure in Clay Pots: An Amazon people on the wheel of change.* Palm Desert, CA/Dallas, TX: Person to Person Books, 306 pp.

Larson, Mildred L. 1998. *Meaning-Based Translation.* Dallas: Summer Institute of Linguistics, 586 pp.

Larson, Mildred. 1998. Meaning-Based Translation Workbook – Biblical Exercises. Dallas: Summer Institute of Linguistics, 307 pp.

Ritter, Gerhard. 1986. "Exposición de algunos elementos de la cultura cashibo-cacataibo." Trabajo monográfico. En cumplimento parcial de las requisitos para optar el título de Maestría en Arte de Misiología. Korntal, Alemania: Freie Hochschule für Mission.

Shell, Olive A. 1950. "Cashibo I: Phonemes." *International Journal of American Linguistics* 16:198-202.

_____. 1957. "Cashibo II: Grammemic analysis of transitive and intransitive verb patterns." *International Journal of American Linguistics* 23:179-218.

_____. 1959. *Vocabulario cashibo-castellano.* Yarinacocha, Peru: Summer Institute of Linguistics (Instituto Lingüístico de Verano).

_____. 1965. "Pano Reconstruction." Ph.D. dissertation, University of Pennsylvania. Published in Spanish as: *Estudios panos 3: Las lenguas pano y su reconstrucción*. Yarinacocha, Perú: Instituto Lingüístico de Verano.

Tessmann, Günter. 1930. Die Indianer Nordost-Perus. Hamburg: Friederichsen, de Gruyter and Co. m.b.h.

Tuggy, Sheila C. 1985. "Candoshi Behavioral Change," in *Five Amazonian Studies*. Dallas, TX: International Museum of Cultures, Publication 19, pp. 5-40. William R. Merrifield, Editor and Desmond C. Derbyshire, General Editor.

Wallis, Ethel Emily. 1965. *Tariri: My Story—From jungle killer to Christian missionary*, as told to Ethel Emily Wallis. New York: Harper & Row.

Wistrand [Robinson], Lila. 1965. "A type of Cashibo moral judgment." *American Anthropologist* 67:1521.

_____. 1968a. "Desorganización y revitalización de los cashibo." *América Indígena* 28:611-18.

_____. 1968b. "Cashibo relative clause constructions." Unpublished M.A. Thesis, University of Texas at Austin, 81 pp.

_____. 1969a. "Folkloric and linguistic analyses of Cashibo narrative prose." Unpublished Ph.D. dissertation. University of Texas at Austin, 359 pp.

_____. 1969b. "Un texto cashibo: El proceso de cremación." *América Indígena* 29:1029-38.

_____. 1969c. "Music and song texts of Amazonian Indians." *Ethnomusicology* 13:469-88.

_____. 1970. "Bilingual jungle school." *Americas* 22 (8): 2-8. "En jíbaro y en castellano" (Spanish edition) 22 (9): 2-8.

_____. 1971a. "Cashibo verb stems, causatives, and proposition consolidation." *Papers from the Fifth Kansas Linguistic Conference*. Lawrence, KS: University of Kansas, 204-13.

Wistrand-Robinson, Lila. 1971b. Review of: *Classification of South American Indian languages* by Cestmir Loukotka, in Johannes Wilbert (ed.), *Linguistics* 75:106-13.

_____. 1972. "A South American Indian Orpheus tale." *Journal of American Folklore* 85:181-83 (April-June).

_____. 1973. "Cashibo T-shaped stone axes." *Journal of the Steward Anthropological Society* (Fall issue), 83-89. University of Illinois.

_____. 1975. "Notas etnográficas sobre los cashibo." *Folklore Americano* (Dec. 1975), 117-40.

_____. 1976. "Some generative solutions to problems in Cashibo phonology." *A. A. Hill Festschrift* 1:287-95. Netherlands: Peter de Ritter Publisher.

_____. 1977. "Cashibo song poetry." *Yearbook for Inter-American Musical Research* 11:137-51. Austin: University of Texas. (Also in: "La poesía de las canciones cashibos." *Datos Etnolingüísticos*. Yarinacocha, Peru: Summer Institute of Linguistics [Instituto Lingüístico de Verano].)

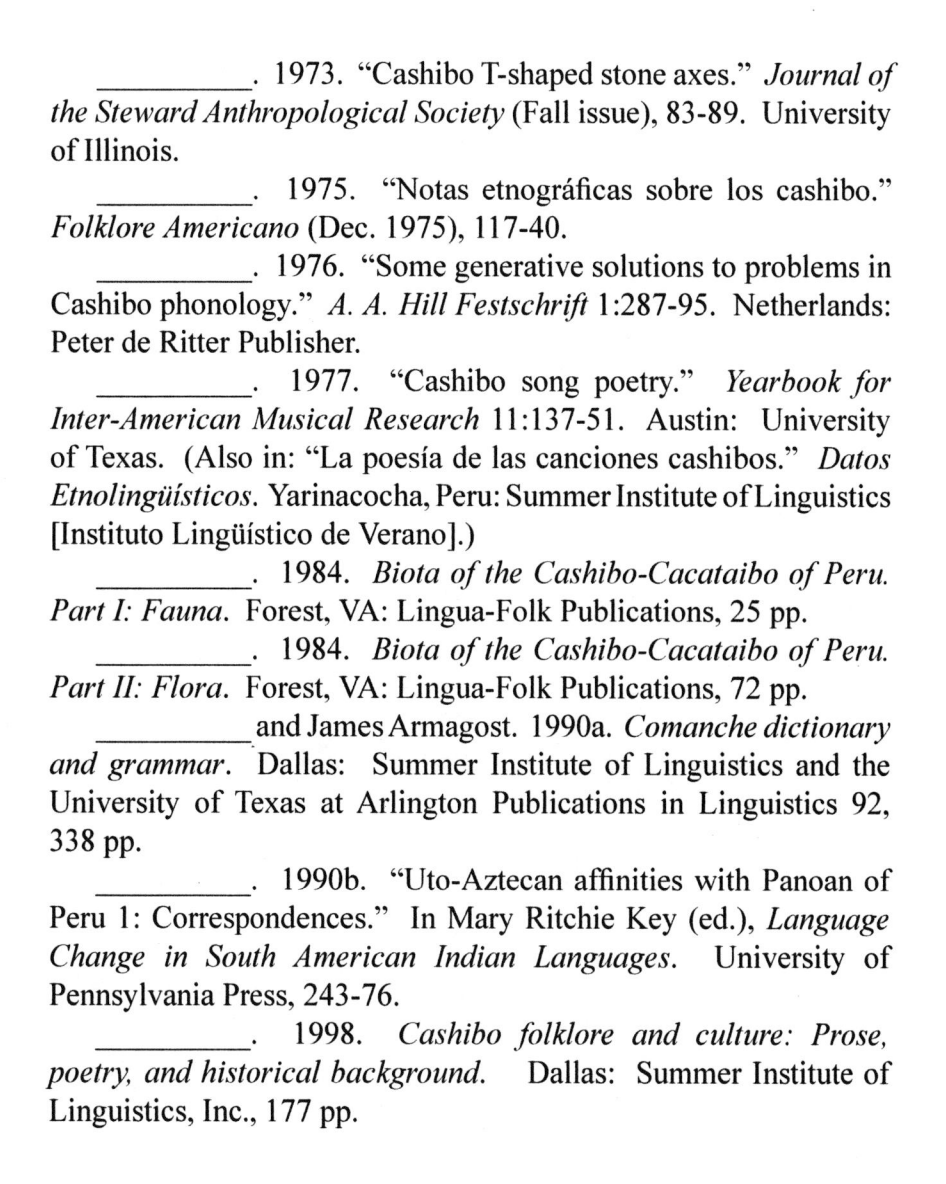

_____. 1984. *Biota of the Cashibo-Cacataibo of Peru. Part I: Fauna*. Forest, VA: Lingua-Folk Publications, 25 pp.

_____. 1984. *Biota of the Cashibo-Cacataibo of Peru. Part II: Flora*. Forest, VA: Lingua-Folk Publications, 72 pp.

_____ and James Armagost. 1990a. *Comanche dictionary and grammar*. Dallas: Summer Institute of Linguistics and the University of Texas at Arlington Publications in Linguistics 92, 338 pp.

_____. 1990b. "Uto-Aztecan affinities with Panoan of Peru 1: Correspondences." In Mary Ritchie Key (ed.), *Language Change in South American Indian Languages*. University of Pennsylvania Press, 243-76.

_____. 1998. *Cashibo folklore and culture: Prose, poetry, and historical background*. Dallas: Summer Institute of Linguistics, Inc., 177 pp.